W9-BQL-416

ICELAND
The First American Republic

This Icelandic Kver is called Geysir, "The Gusher." From it are named the geysers

ICELAND

THE FIRST AMERICAN REPUBLIC

Vilhjalmur Stefansson

GREENWOOD PRESS, PUBLISHERS
WESTPORT, CONNECTICUT

Preface

VILHJALMUR STEFANSSON *is a great explorer, a fine student and an able author. No one is better fitted to write on Iceland, as this book proves.*
Few countries in the world have the romance of Iceland. Lying as it does far to the north, beyond the Ultima Thule of the ancients, it is not a country that attracted those in search of a soft living. It has deserts and glaciers. Its natural resources are few. Its climate is harsh. Only one third of the island can be utilized by man. It is a country for hardy men and women.
Those who migrate to new nations often go in search of an easier life. Take, for example, our own country, the United States. Undoubtedly many, particularly in the early days, came here willing to face hardship and danger for the sake of freedom and opportunity. As our country grew in wealth this picture changed. We did not represent danger and hardship any more, but rather wealth. We were the land where dollars flowed like water. The appeal was to those who wished to get rich and live soft.
In Iceland this has never been the case. Her first set-

*tlers, the Irish, came there in search of solitude. The real
stock, however, was the Scandinavian. They came because they were adventurous, because they wanted their
own land, because they were not afraid to work. Never
at any time was Iceland a country flowing with milk and
honey.*

*The people of Iceland today are in vast majority de-
scended from these Norsemen and deep bred in the Icelandic character are their virtues and strength. Sea wan-
derers by tradition, it is they who struck west first and
reached first Greenland and then the American continent.
Today we sail in great liners with every modern con-
venience, floating hotels on which the feeblest can travel
in comfort. In those days the Norsemen used tiny open
boats. The men who manned them were drenched by the
rain, frozen in the snow and the spray, and scorched by
the sun. Their motive power was a square sail and oars,
but the shadow of their dragon prows passed over much
of the world's seaboard.*

*Poetry is deeply embedded in the Icelandic character.
Their sagas are among the most beautiful ever written.
Those dealing with their discovery and attempted colonization of this country are particularly vivid. There is
breadth to them and the grandeur of simplicity. The
very name they gave to the place where they landed,
Wineland the Good, has a ring to it. To me the description of the struggle that was made by that handful to
establish itself is dramatic, particularly so for the honesty
of the account. It would seem that the most hopeful
attempt failed because of the women. They brought too
few. Bitter jealousies arose. I like particularly the touch
where the Skraeling (Indians) were routed by the bellowing of the bull.*

These sagas on the discovery of America are but a few of the many that form the background of Iceland. There are many others I like, such as the Tale of Gisli, the Outlaw. I spoke of the lack of natural resources in Iceland. There was one product for which they were famous in medieval times. When hawking was the sport of kings and emperors the falcon esteemed over all others was Icelandic. A gift is recorded of Icelandic falcons to Saladin, the Saracen.

But there is another side to Iceland as romantic as any Viking raid. It is the development of the nation as a modern democracy. Iceland, like its Scandinavian cousins, has gone far toward solving the great problems of democracy that are vexing the United States. In Iceland no one is very wealthy and by the same token no one is very poor. The co-operatives, which have proved so successful in other Scandinavian countries, have been developed with equally excellent results. The Icelanders believe as we do in the United States that every citizen must be educated properly and that no one should be allowed to tyrannize and impoverish his fellow citizen. They maintain that the state owes every man an opportunity to make a living. They couple with this the very necessary corollary that everyone must work if work is obtainable and only grant direct relief to those who are incapacitated or who cannot find work. This nation of less than 120,000, set apart from the world upon an island in the North Atlantic, is a laboratory within which "advanced" plans of social betterment have been tried out, and many of them with success. The Icelandic democracy may be studied with profit by Americans today.

THEODORE ROOSEVELT

Contents

Illustrations

xi

Introductory Statement on the First and Second American Republics

THERE IS much in common, though perhaps more in contrast, between the first American democracy and the greatest American democracy.

The republic of Iceland is dated from 930, the year in which sectional governments were replaced by a national parliament. We date the United States either from 1776 or 1789—from the Declaration or from the Constitution —so Iceland became a republic either 846 or 859 years ahead of the United States.

It has been contended that Iceland is part neither of Europe nor of America but a midway house between them—or, to use a figure with truer and more picturesque historical meaning, that Iceland is a stepping stone between the Old and the New worlds.

By the convention of eastern and western hemispheres Iceland comes near being a halfway mark; for the line between them is usually drawn through Iceland. That line, however, cuts east of the middle of the island, and there are textbooks which show part of Iceland on the map of the eastern hemisphere but all of it on the map of the western.

xiii

To reach Iceland from Europe you must cross a wide sea, long out of sight of land—the distance is more than 500 miles from southeastern Iceland to the nearest large European island, Scotland. But from northwestern Iceland children at play see Greenland when they scramble up the mountains that are only 180 miles from the still higher mountains of the Blosseville coast. In northwestern Greenland you do not have to climb a hill to see the next island west, which is Ellesmere—you do not even have to sail to it, but can walk across, as many Europeans and Americans have done the last hundred years, and as the Eskimos have been doing for one or more thousands of years.

The geographers, then, have Iceland American.

It has been said that, although geographically a part of America, Iceland is culturally a part of Europe and should be classed as a European republic, the first north of the Alps. But if culture is to be the standard, what republic is American? Not the United States, for even Will Rogers spoke English, a European language, and dressed, except on rare occasions, much more like an Englishman than like a Cherokee.

The civilization of the United States is predominantly European, favoring England. The culture of Brazil has a somewhat higher native American tinge but is predominantly European, favoring Portugal. The most American of Western republics is perhaps Mexico, but even that country is strikingly European, favoring Spain.

Thus it is pointless to say that Iceland is European because its culture is European. The logic of that reasoning would force us to say that there are no American nations since the culture of all is European.

The discovery of Iceland was the discovery of America; or, if you like, it was the discovery of the New World.

We used to think we knew the approximate time, and the profession and nationality if not the names and biographies, of the men who first unveiled the New World to the Old, for we knew there were Irish clergy in Iceland before 795 A.D. A few years ago there would have been few objections to our saying that they were the first European discoverers of land west of the Atlantic.

True, there were many centuries during which it was generally believed that the Greeks under Pytheas had discovered Iceland, called by them Ultima Thule, around 325 B.C., thus discovering the New World. But then scholarship swung for a time to the view that Pytheas had sailed from Scotland to Norway, discovering Norway, instead of from Scotland to Iceland, discovering Iceland. Recently, however, scholarship has tended to swing back again. Iceland once more is Ultima Thule to many of us—as it was Ultima Thule, or at least Thule, to Columbus when he was there in 1477.

Columbus is so large a figure in the history of American republics that we stop for a parenthetical remark:

Many at first believed that Columbus was telling the truth when he said, through the testimony of his son Ferdinand, that he had been to Iceland the winter of 1477 and that he had sailed more than 300 miles north beyond Iceland without seeing any ice.[1] But there rose gradually among historians the belief, which grew into

[1]This statement was to Columbus part of an argument, which became a passion with him, that it is a mistake to believe the tropics uninhabitable because of the heat or the Arctic because of the cold.

a conviction, that it was impossible to sail 300 miles north from Iceland in winter without seeing ice. It was believed that the ice would hover only a few miles north of the coast. But the Austrians found when they spent a winter on Jan Mayen Island in 1882–83 (at the very 100-Spanish-league distance north of Iceland which Columbus mentions) that no ice was to be seen throughout the winter when looking south towards Iceland. And now the government of Norway, through the pioneering of Hagbard Ekerold, has had an observatory on Jan Mayen for eighteen years, since 1921. During that whole time no ice has been seen in the direction towards Iceland from Jan Mayen.

The main argument relied upon by those who maintain Columbus, or Ferdinand, was a liar about the voyage of 1477 has thus been pulled from under their feet with a vengeance. Columbus, by the same token, now wears one more laurel, that of having made an Arctic voyage and having brought back information which, had scholars believed it, would have advanced Europe's knowledge of the polar regions by nearly four centuries—would have made it unnecessary for the Austrians to "discover" fifty years ago that the sea between Iceland and Jan Mayen is nearly or quite always free of ice in midwinter.

As we were saying, there would have been fair agreement around 1900 that the Irish discovered the New World about 795 A.D. Today we discuss the following probabilities, among others:

The Irish had been visiting Iceland for centuries before 795. We now incline toward thinking probable that the Venerable Bede (674–735) has at least one reference showing that Iceland was known in his day; a few years ago we thought this improbable. We feel similarly about the probabilities where Adamnan (679–704) tells us in his *Life of St Columba* (521–97) that Cormac visited an uninhabited island in the sea beyond Ireland. We are now predisposed to think not merely that Pytheas visited Iceland around 325 B.C. but also that the implication of his statement is correct—that he was informed about Iceland before he visited it, therefore by the people of the British Isles, who may have been familiar with it a few or even many centuries before.

The background of these probabilities has been shifted only in part by a rechecking of history, as in the case of the voyage of Columbus in 1477 A.D. and of Pytheas around 325 B.C. The great shift in the probabilities has been due rather to the archaeologists than to the old-fashioned historians who relied chiefly on documents.

Students of the Bronze Age, and of the late Stone Age, have many of them come to the view that sailing of the high seas was common thousands of years, or at least a thousand years, before the day of those Phoenicians who were publicized to us until recently in high school and college as the fathers of navigation. A statement of the new archaeologist position was made by A. W. Brögger, Director of the National Museum of Norway, in his presidential address to an international congress of archaeologists at Oslo in 1936. There he treated as an established fact the idea of a golden age of navigation which was at its height surely fifteen hundred years before Christ, and that may have been on a high level for as much as a thousand or even two thousand years before. During this golden age man is pictured as having swarmed over the Atlantic, discovering all the islands and plying between the continents that lie east and west of that ocean.

Of course, demonstrating that there was a golden age of seafaring three or four thousand years ago would not of itself prove American civilization connected with that of Egypt or prove the rock structures on Mr William B. Goodwin's farm in New Hampshire as completely Irish and as far pre-Columbian as he and some of his scholarly advisers believe. But establishing the probability of numerous crossings of the Atlantic before Homer would at least remove the barbs of ridicule from the quivers of those who attack anyone who even suggests it may be worth while to study American remains, whether north or south of the Rio Grande, that appear to have suggestions of both a European origin and of an antiquity not only beyond Columbus in 1492 but also beyond Leif and the year 1000.

But we started to tell about Iceland as an American republic.

It was natural Iceland should be a republic; for, apart from a small number of previous Irish inhabitants, the leaders of the colonization (between 870 and 930) were Norwegian petty kings, earls and miscellaneous nobility who, though willing to rule others, were unwilling to be themselves ruled by a super-king. They had been defeated in war when Norway was being united under Harald the Fair-Haired; they refused not only to pay him taxes but to make him obeisance. So it would have been from the frying pan into the fire if they had submitted to a new king in the new land.

Many Norwegian chiefs came to Iceland by way of Scotland and (chiefly) Ireland, some after their families had spent there one or even two generations during which they had intermarried with the local people. They came accompanied, too, by many of their Irish friends, so that, together with Irish immigration related to the commerce of the next two or three centuries, it is believed by different authorities that the Irish percentage of blood in Iceland is anything from ten to fifty. If you add the highest and lowest estimates and divide by two, getting thirty per cent, you may have an approach to the facts.

In language Iceland was wholly Norwegian. In political institutions it was mainly Norwegian, except that a parliament took the place of the king. In literature, as we discuss more fully in a separate chapter, there was a strong influence from Ireland—strangely enough not so much upon the poetry as upon the prose writings, the sagas.

To those who do their reading in English there are two chief books for an introduction to the government of the Icelandic republic during its early period, and for some indication of what influence Iceland had upon the growth of democratic institutions in Britain and other countries. The first of these, chronologically, is *Studies in History and Jurisprudence* (Oxford, 1901, Vol. 1) by that James Bryce who, as Viscount Bryce, was ambassador to the United States from 1907 to 1912 and who is known to Americans as the author of that classic *The American Commonwealth*. The second is *Pioneers of Freedom* (Boston, 1930), written by Sveinbjorn Johnson, formerly justice of the Supreme Court of North Dakota and now legal counsel of the University and professor of law at the University of Illinois.

The Icelandic republic was strong on its parliamentary

and judicial sides but weak in the executive, so that wise laws justly interpreted were often not enforced. This weakness, together with special circumstances discussed in the chapter on Iceland's history, led in 1261 to union with Norway. By 1261 Iceland had been a republic for 331 years, which is 181 years longer than the United States has yet been a republic (counting from the adoption of the Constitution in 1789). There is the difference, too, that while the colonies which later became American states had been governed from Europe by England since their beginning until the Revolution, the colonies of Iceland, which eventually formed the republic of Iceland, were never governed from Europe, either by Norway or any other country, at any time from the start of the large-scale immigration in 870 to the founding of the parliament in 930. Iceland thus had from its beginning as a nation a history of complete independence for 391 years.

It was during the republic that Iceland won its preeminence in literature. While European lands were becoming so Christian that they lost interest in their previous religion, and so mechanized along Christian lines that the efforts to destroy the documents of the old religion were successful, Iceland, although formally Christian, retained its scholarly and popular care for the old religion and wrote its main documents into books. Chief among them are the poetic Edda, of unknown authorship, and the prose Edda, written by Snorri Sturluson (1178–1241) who is referred to by many scholars as the greatest historian of the Middle Ages.

Snorri contributed to the history of practically all the "known world." He and the rest of the saga writers tell of things that happened in Constantinople and on the Barbary Coast, and they give information about the development of the Russian Empire. England, Scotland, Ireland and Germany must go to Iceland for elements of their own history, while the early history of the Scandinavian countries, particularly of Norway, is taught in their schools today largely from the work of Icelandic writers.

Not only must Europe go to Iceland for this knowledge, in greater or less part, but we Americans must also derive from Iceland the first written account of a voyage to our shores, further narration of attempted colonization of our mainland five centuries before Columbus, and the story of the establishment of the second American republic, that of Greenland.

Iceland is, as said, a part of America, or at least of the New World. Greenland, if you look upon the map, is even more intimately connected than is Cuba, or any island of the West Indies, all of which are recognized as parts of America.

Because this chapter is an introduction to a whole book on Iceland it touches upon Icelandic matters briefly and casually. We must deal here somewhat more specifically with Greenland, for it is so related to Iceland that it cannot be ignored without serious loss to our main story.

It may have been children at play who discovered Greenland when they looked northwest from Iceland; but our first record is from a navigator, Gunnbjörn, who, sailing north along the west coast of Iceland, noticed land to the west. That was about the year 900.

For the three years 982–85 we have from a dozen sources in Icelandic literature, and particularly from

Eiríks Saga Rauda (The Narrative of Eirik the Red), the first account in any literature of an Arctic voyage, in the sense of coping systematically with polar conditions, including drifting ice at sea. For Pytheas merely saw ice and turned back. Besides, Pytheas likely enough went to Iceland (if Iceland was Thule) because the British told him of it; he seemingly had a good deal of information about it—he may have traveled with a guide, as many "explorers" have done since. But Eirik went on nothing but the report that land had been seen to the west and on a desire to explore it.

After three years of exploration (982–85), which took him as far up the west coast of Greenland as modern Disko, Lat. 69° 30′ N., he decided to attempt securing colonists, and became not merely the founder of the second American republic but also the first American realtor. For the saga has it that he considered "people would all the more desire to migrate to this land if it had an attractive name; and so he called it Green Land"—thus foreshadowing American real estate "development" and American sales promotion.

It was through the Icelandic republic of Greenland that a man born in Iceland, but then a citizen of Greenland, discovered the mainland of North America. Norway shares in the credit of that discovery about as the British Isles share in the record of John Paul Jones and George Washington, through blood.

There are several stages in the tale of nationalistic credit for successive steps that led to the finding of the American mainland.

Eirik, a child of Norwegian parents, left Norway when his father was exiled—from the record it appears that this was a permanent exile. Leif, Eirik's son, born in Iceland,

left the country first, we might say, by compulsion, when
his father was exiled for three years; and later by choice
when, after the exile, Eirik returned to Iceland, spent the
winter in recruiting colonists, and returned to Greenland
the summer of 986 with about four hundred emigrants
who settled along the west coast from Cape Farewell to
and beyond the present Godthaab, Lat. 64° 15′ N.

The Greenland republic was established about 990,
modeled on the republic of Iceland.

The spring of the year 1000 Leif, who had been visiting in Norway, sailed for Greenland, essentially to return home, though he carried with him two missionaries
for the purpose of converting the Greenlanders formally
—many of the Greenlanders were Christian already, more
or less, through Irish influences.

Previous Greenland voyages had been from Norway
to Iceland, from Iceland to the sighting of east Greenland, and then skirting south around Farewell to the
settlements on the west coast. But Leif was in a hurry,
steered direct for Cape Farewell, missed it in thick
weather and found himself against an eastward-facing
shore where the land had trees on it. There are no trees
on the eastward shore of Greenland. Knowing he had
oversailed the mark, Leif turned northeast. They reached
home while parliament was still in session. The priests
had a chance to argue their case and to secure a vote
before adjournment that the country should be officially
Christian. Thus were the first sighting of the American
mainland and either the first or second step of Christianity
in the New World accomplished in one year.

Our doubt on Christian priorities is because the Icelandic parliament also voted for Christianity the summer
of 1000. As we do not know exact dates for the decisions

of the two governments, we cannot be sure whether it was the first or the second American republic that became the first Christian nation in the New World.

The good fortune of historians is that the conversion of the two lands brought into the field the chief literary organization of western civilization of those days, the clergy of the Church of Rome.

Just possibly what Leif reached in the year 1000 was Newfoundland; not impossibly it was the mainland in Nova Scotia. Almost certainly it was Labrador.

The attempts to colonize the American mainland that are known to us in detail from written history all took place during the first quarter of the eleventh century. The chief of these was by the Icelander Thorfinn Karlsefni, who spent a winter with Eirik in Greenland, apparently 1003–04, and sailed the next summer with three ships and 160 people mainly from Iceland though some of them were from Greenland. The voyage, as had to be the case from Iceland, was by people of Norwegian and, secondarily, of Irish blood; but there are known to have been other nationalities, among them two Germans.

Karlsefni first sailed up the Greenland coast to Disko, which they called Bear Island. Thereon hinges one of the controversies of the scholars.

The sagas always speak of the coast from Farewell to Disko as running east and west; we think of it as running north and south. In fact, it runs southeast-northwest. There is a parallel to this verbal usage where most Americans of the Middle West think of Maine as being north of New York and Connecticut while the local feeling is that Maine is east ("Way down east")—the truth being that it is northeast. Failing to apply this principle to

Greenland, historians have found it difficult to explain how in two days of sailing "south" from Disko, or from any other point on the west coast of Greenland, you could reach land in America. This difficulty vanishes when you realize that if in the Greenlandic use of the Icelandic language northwest was west, then by the same usage southwest had to be called south.

It is the usage of Greenland and not the usage of Iceland that is being written when the Icelandic saga narrator tells us that Karlsefni sailed six days south and struck Helluland. Six days "south" (i.e., southwest) is just about the average speed for ships of the period to cover the distance from Disko to Baffin Island—which, then, is Helluland of the saga, the Land of Flat Stones.

Progressing south, Karlsefni came to Markland, the Land of Forest, which is southern Labrador and Newfoundland, perhaps running into the Gulf of St Lawrence and perhaps extending south to or past Nova Scotia. Then, either in the southern Gulf of St Lawrence, as has recently been maintained, or, according to the more numerous view, along the New England coast to New York and beyond, was Vinland, the Land of Wine or the Land of Wineberries.

In the argument that Vinland, Land of Wine, cannot have been farther north than grapes grow it has been insisted that *vinber* must be translated grapes; but that is not necessary. For any berries from which wine is made are called wineberries to this day in Norway and may very well have been called wineberries in Iceland and Greenland during the Middle Ages.

The first natives whom the Icelanders met in Labrador were clearly Eskimos. Those with whom they had fights later on may have been Eskimos, for this people probably extended farther south then than now—they are believed to have run at one time at least as far south as a third of the way down the Newfoundland coast. More likely they were Algonquins or other non-Eskimo Indians.

In any case, the hostility of the natives drove the Icelandic colonists away. They had battles and were victorious but lost some of their people and realized that they could not maintain themselves permanently. They had small advantage in fighting equipment. They did have armor, but their bows and arrows were little or no better than those of the native Americans—there was no such superiority as the later European colonists had through gunpowder. Besides, Scandinavia had entered a period of depression. The time of their exuberant expansion westward through conquests of northern France and parts of the British Isles, and through colonization, as of the Hebrides, Orkneys, Shetlands, Faroes and Iceland, had spent itself. It was now a time of regression.

Before leaving the subject of the Icelandic and Greenlandic discovery and attempted colonization of the American mainland we might perhaps give a few specimen paragraphs from the long and circumstantial accounts. We take from the saga of Eirik the Red the statement of Karlsefni's navigation. The extract begins where he had spent the winter of 1003–04 as guest of Eirik the Red in southern west Greenland. The expedition sails up the west Greenland shore to Disko (Bear Island), and then southwest and south to Baffin Island, Labrador and the coast southward. We use the translation by Arthur Middleton Reeves from his monumental work of literal translations and documentary facsimiles, *The Finding of Wineland the Good*, London, 1895.

About this time there began to be much talk at Brattahlid,
to the effect that Wineland the Good should be explored,
for, it was said, that country must be possessed of many
goodly qualities. And so it came to pass, that Karlsefni and
Snorri fitted out their ship, for the purpose of going in
search of that country in the spring. Biarni and Thorhall
joined the expedition with their ship, and the men who had
borne them company. There was a man named Thorvard;
he was wedded to Freydis, a natural daughter of Eric the
Red. He also accompanied them, together with Thorvald,
Eric's son, and Thorhall, who was called the Huntsman. He
had been for a long time with Eric as his hunter and fisherman during the summer, and as his steward during the winter. Thorhall was stout and swarthy, and of giant stature;
he was a man of few words, though given to abusive language, when he did speak, and he ever incited Eric to evil.
He was a poor Christian; he had a wide knowledge of the
unsettled regions. He was on the same ship with Thorvard
and Thorvald. They had that ship which Thorbiorn had
brought out. They had in all one hundred and sixty men,
when they sailed to the Western-settlement, and thence to
Bear Island. Thence they bore away to the southward two
days. Then they saw land, and launched a boat, and explored
the land, and found there large flat stones (*hellur*), and
many of these were twelve ells wide; there were many
Arctic foxes there. They gave a name to the country, and
called it Helluland (the land of flat stones). Then they
sailed with northerly winds two days, and land then lay before them, and upon it was a great wood and many wild
beasts; an island lay off the land to the south-east, and there
they found a bear, and they called this Biarney (Bear
Island), while the land where the wood was they called
Markland (Forest-land). Thence they sailed southward
along the land for a long time, and came to a cape; the land
lay upon the starboard; there were long strands and sandy
banks there. They rowed to the land and found upon the

cape there the keel of a ship, and they called it there Kia-larnes (Keelness); they also called the strands Furdustrandir (Wonder-strands), because they were so long to sail by. Then the country became indented with bays, and they steered their ships into a bay. . . .

There follows now an account of how people were sent inland to explore, and of what resources they found —berries, self-sown wheat, etc. The expedition sailed forth; the coastline and topography are described. A place was selected for wintering. The livestock grazed out more successfully during the cold months than if in Greenland or Iceland, but food nevertheless became scarce. A whale was secured and starvation averted.

The literary principle of comic relief is widely applied through the sagas, even the ones most factual—amusing things do happen and the historian may use them, the Icelanders felt. We have a case of this in our narrative where it tells about a difference of opinion between Karlsefni and Thorhall during the second summer of the expedition which led to a split in the company, Thorhall taking one ship and Karlsefni two, the parties going in opposite directions. We follow Thorhall, from the comic to the tragic:

It is said, that Thorhall wished to sail to the northward beyond Wonder-strands, in search of Wineland, while Karlsefni desired to proceed to the southward, off the coast. Thorhall prepared for his voyage out below the island, having only nine men in his party, for all of the remainder of the company went with Karlsefni. And one day when Thorhall was carrying water aboard his ship, and was drinking, he recited this ditty:

> "When I came, these brave men told me,
> Here the best of drink I'd get,

Now with water-pail behold me,—
Wine and I are strangers yet.
Stooping at the spring, I've tested
All the wine this land affords;
Of its vaunted charms divested,
Poor indeed are its rewards."

And when they were ready, they hoisted sail; whereupon
Thorhall recited this ditty:

"Comrades, let us now be faring
Homeward to our own again!
Let us try the sea-steed's daring,
Give the chafing courser rein.
Those who will may bide in quiet,
Let them praise their chosen land,
Feasting on a whale-steak diet,
In their home by Wonder-strand."

Then they sailed away to the northward past Wonder-
strands and Keelness, intending to cruise to the westward
around the cape. They encountered westerly gales, and
were driven ashore in Ireland, where they were grievously
maltreated and thrown into slavery. There Thorhall lost his
life, according to that which traders have related.

The first meeting of Europeans and the natives of
America was on the mainland. For Eirik and his colonists
had seen no people in Greenland, although they had
found old skin boats and other remains which showed (in
the light of their later knowledge and ours) that Eskimos had been there. We dip back into the saga where
the expedition had spent the second winter on the American mainland.

. . . And when spring opened, they discovered, early one
morning, a great number of skin-canoes, rowing from the

south past the cape, so numerous, that it looked as if coals had been scattered broadcast out before the bay; and on every boat staves were waved. Thereupon Karlsefni and his people displayed their shields, and when they came together, they began to barter with each other. Especially did the strangers wish to buy red cloth, for which they offered in exchange peltries and quite grey skins. They also desired to buy swords and spears, but Karlsefni and Snorri forbade this. In exchange for perfect unsullied skins, the Skrellings would take red stuff a span in length, which they would bind around their heads. So their trade went on for a time, until Karlsefni and his people began to grow short of cloth, when they divided it into such narrow pieces, that it was not more than a finger's breadth wide, but the Skrellings still continued to give just as much for this as before, or more.

It so happened, that a bull, which belonged to Karlsefni and his people, ran out from the woods bellowing loudly. This so terrified the Skrellings, that they sped out to their canoes, and then rowed away to the southward along the coast. For three entire weeks nothing more was seen of them. At the end of this time, however, a great multitude of Skrelling boats was discovered approaching from the south, as if a stream were pouring down, and all of their staves were waved in a direction contrary to the course of the sun, and the Skrellings were all uttering loud cries. Thereupon Karlsefni and his men took red shields and displayed them. The Skrellings sprang from their boats, and they met then, and fought together. . . .

The Icelanders won this battle, though losing men. Karlsefni became impressed with the impossibility of keeping a foothold against large numbers, who, as we have said, were almost as well-armed as the Europeans.

The birth of the first American of European descent

is told parenthetically in the closing part of the narrative which gives details that help us understand why it is that so many Icelanders of today have genealogies that run back to the first white child born on the American mainland—Iceland specializes in genealogies, some of which at least are as reliable as some Mayflower genealogies.

. . . Snorri, Karlsefni's son, was born in the first autumn, and he was three winters' old when they took their departure. When they sailed away from Wineland, they had a southerly wind, and so came upon Markland . . .

The following summer Karlsefni sailed to Iceland and Gudrid with him, and he went home to Reyniness. His mother believed that he had made a poor match, and she was not at home the first winter. However, when she became convinced that Gudrid was a very superior woman, she returned to her home, and they lived happily together. Hallfrid was a daughter of Snorri, Karlsefni's son, she was the mother of Bishop Thorlak, Runolf's son. They had a son named Thorbiorn, whose daughter's name was Thorunn, (she was) Bishop Biorn's mother. Thorgeir was the name of a son of Snorri, Karlsefni's son, (he was) the father of Ingveld, mother of Bishop Brand the Elder. Steinunn was a daughter of Snorri, Karlsefni's son, who married Einar, a son of Grunder-Ketil, a son of Thorvald Crook, a son of Thori of Espihol. Their son was Thorstein the Unjust, he was the father of Gudrun, who married Jorund of Keldur. Their daughter was Halla, the mother of Flosi, the father of Valgerd, the mother of Sir Erlend the Stout, the father of Sir Hauk the Lawman. Another daughter of Flosi was Thordis, the mother of Fru Ingigerd the Mighty. Her daughter was Fru Hallbera, Abbess of Reyniness at Stad. Many other great people in Iceland are descended from Karlsefni and Thurid, who are not mentioned here. God be with us, Amen!

The failure to colonize the American mainland did not break the connection between the mainland and Europe through Greenland and Iceland. As we shall see, there is a recorded voyage from Greenland to Labrador and thence to Iceland as late as 1347—which is the last recorded, but not necessarily the last contact.

We give now an outline of the relation of Iceland's sister republic, Greenland, to Europe before Columbus. For it was through Greenland that Iceland, like Europe, had its chief connection with North America during the late Middle Ages.

The Church appointed the first Bishop of Greenland in 1124, making this a separate bishopric under the Archbishop, first of Hamburg, Germany, and later of Nidaros, Norway; the last Greenland bishop was still drawing a salary in the early part of the Reformation when he was captured by the Lutherans in Denmark and died as their prisoner at Maribo Cloister in 1537. So that the bishopric of this American republic well overlaps the journeys of Columbus.

Columbus is thought by some to have at least sighted the eastern coast of Greenland during his early seafaring in the North Atlantic. With little dispute he visited Iceland, and with no dispute he associated with merchants of Bristol, England, who (as we know from a combination of historical and archaeological sources) were frequent visitors to Iceland, at the least occasional visitors to Greenland, and familiar with the Greenlandic and Icelandic knowledge of North America, even if these Bristol men perhaps never themselves went to the American mainland before Columbus. So the bishopric of Greenland not merely overlapped the period of the

Columbus voyages; it can have had direct influence upon the Columbus development.

Greenland, under the name which it still has, Labrador as Markland, Land of Forest, and the coast south of Labrador as Vinland, Land of Wine, first appeared in European literature through the publication of the history of the Archbishopric of Hamburg by Adam of Bremen about 1075. Thereafter the New World, although chiefly the Greenland sector of it, remained in the consciousness of the scholars of Europe. We give only a few of the literary examples.

About 1250 Frederick II, Holy Roman Emperor, King of Sicily and Jerusalem, finished the writing of his great classic, *De Arte Venandi cum Avibus* (The Art of Hunting with Birds), which became as much a best seller as any book could in those pre-printing days, for Europe was more obsessed then with falconry than we are now with baseball. The work contained, in addition to the lore of falconry, broad information in many other fields of knowledge. Through the centuries between Frederick II and Columbus nearly every considerable library in Europe contained this book. In it Frederick II assumes knowledge of Greenland to be so common that it is unnecessary to tell his readers where it is. He feels he locates Iceland satisfactorily by merely saying that it is an island lying in the sea between Norway and Greenland.

Sticking to falconry a bit longer, we mention that during the Crusades the birds from Greenland had special consideration from both the retrievers and the defenders of the Holy Sepulchre. On the Christian side one of the popes gave a special dispensation to the higher clergy who wished to engage in falconry immediately following the celebration of a mass. These princes of the Church were not merely permitted to wear a hunting costume under their priestly robes during the celebration but were also permitted to have their falcons with them and even to let them perch on the altar. We know from other sources that these high prelates favored white falcons. The white falcons were American, for they were from Greenland.

On the Moslem side of the Crusades the appreciation of American falcons was equally keen. Some time before 1396 the Saracens captured a son of the Duke of Burgundy and asked in ransom twelve Greenland falcons. It is a commonplace of the history of falconry that the hawks were never bred in captivity like pigeons but were always captured in the wild. The duke's son was ransomed in 1396, which shows either that there were on hand in Europe at least a dozen hawks that had been captured in Greenland or else that an expedition was sent there to fetch them.

More striking documents are those from the Vatican. In 1276 Pope John XXI and in 1282 Nicholas III wrote letters about the collection of church taxes, tithes, in Greenland. In 1448 Nicholas V wrote that the Christians in Greenland had been attacked thirty years before by barbarians, who had killed many and carried others away in captivity. Now some of the captives had returned to their homes but their poverty was so great that they had been unable to support priests and a bishop. In 1492, when Columbus was on his so widely advertised journey to the West Indies, Pope Alexander VI wrote a letter in which he mentions having been already interested in Greenland while in minor orders, around 1456; having continued his interest when he was a bishop, around

1486; and says that now as pope he continues his interest in the fortunes of that most remote of bishoprics, Greenland. The Christians in Greenland, he had been informed, were so hard up that they were compelled to use fish and milk as substitutes for bread and wine in administering the sacrament.

Doubtless it was not wholly through information from such sources as Bristol merchants but also from the documentary learning of the Church that the kings of Portugal negotiated with the kings of Denmark (from whom they every now and then received presents of Greenland falcons in return for which they sent Denmark cargoes of port wine) for sending the well-known freebooting navigators Pining and Pothorst to explore lands west of the Atlantic in 1476.

Then there were the maps. Green Land (our Greenland), Flat Stone Land (our Baffin Island), the Land of Forest (our southern Labrador with Newfoundland), and the Land of Wine (our New England coast) were usually thought of as separate islands, although the Land of Wine was apparently sometimes considered a mainland connected far to the south with Africa. We cannot enter deep cartographic discussion, and point out merely that these islands, or islands derived at least in part from the stories about them, dot the Atlantic of late medieval cartography, especially through the century just before Columbus.

It has been fashionable lately to derive Brazil, the name of one of these islands and later the name of an American republic, from the Irish word meaning "Land of the Blessed," but for that interpretation there is no basis except in speculation. For a second and at least equally plausible view has it that Brazil is not from the

Irish but from the Iberian languages and that it means "forested." Then Brazil becomes merely a translation into an Iberian language of the Icelandic Markland, Land of Forest. (A part of this argument is that one of the Azores used to be called Brazil and was so called because it was the most wooded of that group of islands. Students of cartography do not confuse this Brazil with the other Brazil which lay farther north and west, the one which the school of thought we now discuss considers to have been called Brazil as a literal translation from the Icelandic word Markland.)

There can be much argument on whence came the islands that lay to the west of Europe on the maps familiar to Columbus; but on some there is no dispute. The Dane Claudius Clavus, familiar with Greenland from Scandinavian hearsay, drew in Italy, where the Church knew Greenland through the administration of its bishopric, a map showing Greenland that was not published until 1835, although it is usually assigned to the year 1424. However, a map which he drew in 1430 began to circulate through the Latin countries at once and was printed in the Ulm 1482 edition of Ptolemy's geography. This shows Greenland in its approximate proper shape and in its right position as viewed from Europe.

These things we know from the documents we have cited. There is background for them and local color in the extensive literature of Iceland. In the saga period, however, books dealt chiefly with the deeds of nobles and their retainers, little with the affairs of the common man. Later, when the sagas were replaced by annals written in the cloisters, and because the authentic heroic period was over, we find chiefly notations on miracles, shipwrecks, plagues and famines.

An entry of 1347 tells of a Greenlandic ship which had been to Markland being wrecked in Iceland. Most commentators on this entry have agreed, whether Icelandic or foreign, that the scribe would have entered something about the voyage having been extraordinary had it been extraordinary. The notation, therefore, shows that three-cornered voyages from Greenland to Labrador, Labrador to Iceland and Iceland to Greenland were a commonplace as late as 1347. The ships would be going to the mainland for timber; they would sell the wood in Iceland and thereby purchase European wares for use in Greenland.

We do not deal here with the vicissitudes of the Greenland colony and how it gradually disappeared, in one of two ways—some think the colonists were killed off by Eskimos while others believe that they intermarried with the Eskimos and lost their European culture after a breakdown of Greenland's own shipping, which is supposed to have come soon after the period when the mentioned shipwreck took place in Iceland.

This introduction is no history of the pre-Columbian relation which Iceland maintained with Europe on the east and with Greenland and more remote parts of the New World on the west. We are merely attempting to focus a bit of added attention on the fact that there exists a wealth of reliable historical material upon the pre-Columbian unveiling of the New World to Europe, upon the first American republic, the second American republic, and the role they played in four fields, among others: the introduction of democracy into the New World; the introduction of Christianity; the building of the first written American literature of European descent; and the maintenance of a contact between the Old and

New worlds, perhaps from very early times but at least from Dicuil's account for 795 to the Lindbergh voyage of Columbus in 1492.

ICELAND

The First American Republic

CHAPTER I

Iceland and Its History

THE ICELANDIC NATION seems to be the only one in the
world which can trace its history back to its very beginning and also through more than a thousand years. For
it was settled within historic times; there were no
aborigines when the Irish priests arrived; there were
none there but Irish when the Norse vikings arrived,
and the early Norse settlers had a lively interest in history
and genealogy. True enough, there are gaps; but many
an Icelander of today can trace his ancestry back through
ten centuries—and some farther, to chieftains or royalty
in Norway or in Ireland.

In the Introduction we have outlined the position of
Iceland as a steppingstone between two worlds. In view
of its historic and geographic connection with America
it may appear strange that comparatively few Americans
know where and what it is.

It would seem high time that the United States and
Canada discover the nation that discovered the mainland
of North America.

Iceland is the fourth largest island of the North Atlantic, after Greenland, Britain and Newfoundland. It lies between 63° 24′ and 66° 32′ north latitude, with its north coast just touching the Arctic Circle. The area is about 40,000 square miles, a fifth larger than Ireland, a fifth smaller than Pennsylvania. But while Ireland has a population of over 4,000,000 and Pennsylvania nearly 10,000,000, Iceland's population is only 120,000.

In the Introduction we have discussed the Irish occupation of the island while it was called Thule, or Ultima Thule. It has had several other names. It was called Snowland by Naddod, the first Norwegian who reached it, and Gardar's Holm after a Swede named Gardar who sailed around it. Its present name comes from a disgruntled Norwegian viking, Floki Vilgerdarson who, through incompetence and neglect, had lost his livestock during the winter of 865–866. Floki's unfavorable reports, however, seem to have carried little weight with his countrymen who were as ready to believe the statement of one of his companions that the "grass was dewy with butter."

The tidings of the Norse "discovery" of what the Irish (and, no doubt, the Scots and the English) had long known, spread rapidly through northwestern Europe. The times were restless, particularly in Norway where Harald the Fair-Haired had set out to unify Scandinavia in the manner successful with Charlemagne to the south. In the battle of Hafursfjord he had broken the power of the nobility and the petty kings; but he had not broken their spirit and, rather than bow to his victory, many sought freedom in exile.

The history of the time is lively and at times gruesome with the tales of these exiled, plundering vikings, of their descents upon England, Ireland and France. Here we are concerned particularly with those of the vikings who settled in Ireland, northern Scotland, the Orkneys, Shetlands and Hebrides; for after remaining from a year or two to a generation or two, many left for Iceland, some taking with them a retinue of Celts. Other vikings turned their prows directly westward from Norway. At first Harald was seemingly glad to be rid of these self-exiled malcontents, but their growing numbers finally alarmed him and he imposed a visa charge of four ounces of silver on each person who left Norway to settle in Iceland.

It is a coincidence that Iceland's first permanent settler, Ingolf Arnarson, made his home where the capital city, Reykjavik, now stands. Together with his comrade in arms, Hjörleif, he had previously made a survey of the island and had then returned to Norway. Their uncomfortable Norwegian situation as petty royalty and the good opinion they had formed of Iceland led these two chieftains to move their households westward.

When Ingolf sighted land on his second voyage he threw overboard the sacred columns of his high-seat, declaring that he would settle wherever the gods deigned to cast them ashore. The two parties landed in different places on the south coast to spend the first winter. That season Hjörleif was murdered by some Irish thralls he had brought with him. Ingolf's search for his pillars was rewarded after three years, for at last he found them in what is now the bay of Reykjavik.[1]

Ingolf, who is looked upon as the father of his country, resembled in many ways the pioneer leaders who won the American West. A gifted man of action, he pulled up stakes in the land he knew and, with his family and friends, set out for another far away. Himself established in the new country, he welcomed and helped newly arriving settlers. For centuries his descendants were looked upon as a sort of Mayflower group.

The date 874 is usually assigned to Ingolf's settling in Iceland. During the following decades there was a steady stream of immigrants. It is poetic justice that Floki was borne westward again with this tide, only to find that with the best lands taken up he now had to be content with rather poor holdings.

Sixty years after the colonization of Reykjavik, the population of Iceland was around 50,000. Practically every district now inhabited was by then settled and the old free and easy system of claiming land was abandoned. Latecomers were either given tracts by those who were before them or else they purchased land.

In the beginning there was little social or political organization; there was no central authority for the country as a whole. But two customs of North Europeans, joint worship at a temple and the calling of freemen's assemblies, helped toward a national union.

[1]Reykja Vik, Bay of Smokes, so called because of the hot springs in the district. In chill and clear weather the steam from these larger and smaller springs is, at a distance, like columns and wisps of smoke.

The most influential man in a district usually built a temple on his farm. It was convenient for other settlers in the neighborhood to gather there for worship and at the same time to bring up matters of common interest. The owner of the temple was both a spiritual and political leader, and by common consent became *godi* (priest-chieftain) for his district. The meetings at his home developed gradually into assemblies, or Things, which became more or less fixed.

In his *Studies in History and Jurisprudence*, Bryce relates these Icelandic assemblies to their collateral British institutions. He says that "This assembly resembled the Old English Folk Mot, and was called the Thing, a name which survives in our English word Hustings (Husting or House Thing), the platform from whence candidates spoke at parliamentary elections, which disappeared in A.D. 1872 when written nominations were prescribed by the statute which introduced vote by ballot." He points out that Thing Vellir (the nominative plural) is more familiar to us as Thing Valla which is the genitive plural —the form which remains in Thingwall (near Liverpool), Tynwald (in the Isle of Man), and Dingwall (in Rosshire).

In Iceland the Things were at first unrelated to each other. But as the population grew the need developed for a larger and more effective organization to prevent sectional quarrels or to legislate for the common good. With the consent of the priest-chiefs a General Assembly, or Althing, was established some sixty years after

the first settlers arrived. Ulfljot, an Icelander of prominence, went to Norway where he consulted learned men
and received advice about making up a code of law. His
foster brother, Grimur Geitskör (goat beard) traveled
in the meantime over the whole country preparing the
people for the coming event and looking for a suitable
place to hold the meeting.

In the summer of 930 the Althing was established at
Thingvellir (the Plains of Assembly) and Iceland became an organized commonwealth. As Bryce points out,
this commonwealth differed from most other states in
that it did not grow naturally from small beginnings but
was deliberately established by the agreement of independent groups of men who were seeking to attain the
common ends of justice and order. Thus, when Athelstan
the Victorious of England was fighting Scots and North-
umbrians, when Henry the Fowler was repelling the
Magyars, and when the Carolingians were on the wane in
Gaul, the people of Iceland, with deliberate intent and
without bloodshed created for themselves a republic.

In the new parliament there were two chief offices.
One, the General Godi, was honorary and hereditary.
Of more practical importance was the Speaker whose
duty it was to recite aloud before the assembly the whole
law of Iceland, going through it in the course of his three-
year term. Once every year he had to recite the formulas
of actions-at-law. He was bound to answer every question concerning the provisions of the law but was not
required to advise applicants what course they should

pursue. When questions for legal ruling arose they were referred to him and his decision was final.

The real power, however, was vested in the godis who were the only voting members of the legislative body. They numbered thirty-six; but when legislation was being passed each godi had two advisers. Later, for political reasons, this number of 108 was increased to 144.

With some analogy to the states of the United States, Iceland was divided into four districts, each of which had its Quarter Thing, like a state legislature, for settling local matters. Cases involving disputes between Things and amendments to the constitution were brought before the Althing at the annual meeting in June.

The Althing served as a court of last appeal, being, in that respect, similar to the later English House of Lords.

Although most fundamentally resembling institutions like the British Parliament and the American Congress, Althing had much in common with what we think of as an American institution of recent date, the Chautauqua. The Althing was not like the itinerant sequence of half a dozen brown tent groups of entertainers and informants that used to move through our villages; it resembled more the parent institution at Chautauqua Lake, New York State, and the numerous chautauquas of that type which flourished exuberantly at the beginning of our century and some of which, including the New York Chautauqua, are still going concerns.

All the roads of the Icelandic republic led to the Al-

thing—mere bridle paths they were, which took direction
from the gaps in the mountains and the fordable places in
the rivers. During late spring parties in festive mood,
though sometimes concerned also with grave matters such
as the institution or defense of a lawsuit, would start moving towards their focus in the southwest, about twenty
miles inland from Reykjavik. Arrived at the Plains of the
Althing, Thingvellir, those chieftains who attended regu-
larly would pitch camp in their accustomed places; the
rest tented where they could find room or according
to friendship with those whose locations were established.

During the protracted session there was much visiting
back and forth between the camps, retailing of gossip,
spreading and trading of home news. More important,
there would be occasions when men just returned from
abroad were given a formal hearing, and there were
many occasions when fortunate groups listened to these
travelers privately. A chieftain was back from successful
piracy, even perhaps from North Africa or the eastern
Mediterranean. A poet was home from being laureate
several years at a court of one of the European kings.
There would be a soldier returned to live in Iceland after
a decade as member of the bodyguard of the Emperor
of the East, or of some lesser majesty. Each had a story
worth telling; some were masters of the storytellers' art.

For orderly but truthful relation was in this period
more highly esteemed than perhaps any of the other arts,
unless it were poetry. The narrator, however skillful, was
required as a matter of honor and of his own safety to

Thingvellir—The Plains of Assembly.

relate things so accurately that none of his audience could check him up—some of them as conversant with the matter as himself and listening ready for a verbal challenge, or a challenge to a duel if the falsehood appeared serious.

To a degree the Althing was also a trading fair; a national exposition. We read more of the exchange of princely gifts than of straight commercial transactions; but that may be in part for the reason we have mentioned, that the sagas deal chiefly with the doings of the nobility and only in rare cases with those of the common people. There were courtships naturally, though we hear of them in the main only when they were formal—where a chieftain with his son, accompanied by clansmen, retainers and friends, would pay a state visit to another chieftain, asking the hand of a daughter or other kinswoman. The sagas describe the costumes worn by ladies of prominence and by girls that were betrothed. They describe, too, the garb of men who were prominent. So the Althing must have been a disseminator of fashions. Travelers from remote lands evidently brought there not merely cloth that was precious but also new ideas for the cut of garments.

Still it would seem that fashion in dress changed only a little more during a century of the Iceland republic than had been the case during a century of the Athenian republic—not more than our fashions nowadays change in a year.

Many things were provided for in the constitution, but there was no provision for a federal executive authority. The carrying out of a sentence was in the hands of the person successful in a lawsuit, who was assisted by his local godi. The system functioned on respect for the law and on the balance of power between the most influential families. This might seem a rather unsuitable foundation on which to build a state, but the state so built lasted for more than three centuries. Icelanders have always felt, and still feel, that national life reached its highest level during the period of what now would be considered near-anarchy.

In comparison with other countries Iceland was peaceful during this time. There were feuds but no wars. Legislation was progressive. Duels were prohibited as early as 1006. Even at that early date within each district mutual insurance provided against fire and other heavy losses of property. The laws covered a wide field. Marriage, divorce, inheritance, distribution of property, regulation of weights and measures, all had separate provisions. There was a criminal code with punishment by graduated fine for every offense except parricide, for the nature of this crime rendered its commission unthinkable. Three centuries earlier than in England, trial by jury was inaugurated. Sir George Webbe Dasent, himself an Englishman, points out that it was from Iceland that England received not only this "bulwark of Englishmen's rights" but also the special demurrers and other subtleties of pleading.

After seventy years of the republic Christianity achieved in Iceland one of the bloodless victories that were rare during the conversion of the Scandinavian peoples. The religion had already been practised by Celtic members of the Icelandic community and by a few who were of Norwegian descent. But it had made little headway, and that little chiefly among women. In fact, one of the new religion's chief handicaps was that it was considered effeminate.

If you read but casually the history of this period you feel bewildered at the sudden vote by Althing in the year 1000 to make the land Christian. There have been several explanations; or rather, there are explanations which combine several factors in varying degree. We mention two of them.

In this period Norway was the most aggressive land in northwestern Europe and had for king a passionate soldier of the Cross, Olaf Tryggvason. It has been said of him that he would dispatch missionaries to a community one year and, if they failed, would send an army the next. So it was a choice of a baptism of water or of blood and water. There were spokesmen for him in Iceland, urging conversion. There were some Icelandic leaders who feared the arrival of a battle fleet that would attempt to make Iceland both Christian and a province of Norway. The chance of that could be decreased, or the issue postponed, by not giving Olaf a religious motive for visiting Iceland.

It is the more difficult to arrive now at a conclusion of this argument because Olaf was defeated in Norway that year at the Battle of Svold, with loss of life as well as of kingdom. So it is wholly speculative what he might have tried to do with regard to Iceland.

Hermannsson considers that the main impetus toward Christianity came through the discontent of prominent Icelanders with the amount of influence the godis wielded —it was felt that a change in religion would be a way to diminish their power. When a strong pro-Christian feeling began to develop there developed, too, a strong anti-Christian sentiment, for the new religion was viewed as a Norwegian import and as such to be distrusted. The godis naturally saw in the new belief a threat to their spiritual-temporal power. At one point it seemed as if a general upheaval or civil war might break upon the country. The wisest, however, foreseeing ruin, brought about a compromise. The new faith was legally introduced, but the constitution remained unchanged. The godis won a political victory the while they suffered a religious defeat.

This wholesale conversion did not for a time affect the people greatly, for their new religious activities mainly concerned the changing of pagan temples into 'churches and the adoption of holy orders by some of the young men. Helgi the Lean was perhaps a typical convert. He renamed his homestead Kristnes, in honor of Christ; but for sea voyages he sacrificed to and worshiped Thor.

In the beginning foreign bishops came to Iceland. Gizur the White, who had been a leader in making Christianity the official religion, was among those who did not like to see church affairs administered by foreigners. His son, Isleif, became the first native bishop, in 1056. He had much to contend with. His income was small and his congregation was not submissive, partly because the foreign bishops were more lenient than he. Eventually an order from the Archbishop of Bremen forbade the people to have any dealings with the foreign primates; but Isleif's lot seems not to have improved much; for, asked on his deathbed to name his successor, he replied that he did not know anyone who would be willing to accept such an offer unless better treatment were given him.

The second bishop, Gizur, son of Isleif, was a man of accomplishments and was dearly beloved, but he was often away on long travels and even engaged in commercial enterprises. However, he did improve the lot of the clergy; for he, and other influential contemporaries, persuaded the Althing to pass the law of tithes by which one part went to the bishop, one to the churches, one to the clergy and one to the poor. Gizur's bishopric was at Skalholt. It was felt that the country could support two bishoprics, so another was created at Holar in 1106.

The turbulent and picturesque Saga Age was the sixty-year period of the colonization and then the first hundred years of the republic to about 1030. There had been, first, the stirring events of the colonization itself. Next there had been the discovery and colonization of Greenland; then the discovery, exploration and attempted colonization of the mainland of North America. However, the voyages to Greenland, Labrador and south through the Gulf of St Lawrence and down the New England coast stir our imagination nowadays disproportionately. In the minds of the Icelanders they took a level with the rest of their adventures—the voyages through the Baltic and to Russia; the foraging raids down the coasts of Spain and into the Mediterranean; the service of Icelanders as laureates and bodyguards at various courts; their journeys to and through every known land and sea of the time, usually to come back home and spend the later years in reminiscence.

After 1030 come what are thought of in Iceland as the two centuries of peace, when commerce replaced piracy. The most fashionable journeys now were pilgrimages to the Holy Land, although there continued to be much quiet travel to many countries. It was in this placid time that the sagas took the varied forms which they now have in the vellum manuscripts—as sober family histories and national histories of Iceland and of various European countries, chiefly those of the northwest; as more or less romanticized adventures of the leaders of the saga period; as highly fictionized and decorated sagas of the Burnt Njal type which are historical novels rather than histories. There was in this period also the recording of the ancient poetry and mythology which the settlers had brought with them, mostly from the Scandinavian countries, although some of it colored through other influences, chiefly Irish.

In the latter part of the twelfth century the balance of power between the influential families gradually became disturbed. The offices of priest-chiefs were gathered into the hands of men who started bloody feuds with each other. Mackenzie considers that, left to themselves, the Icelanders might have resolved their quarrels, but that concealed interference of Norwegians "while aggravating internal evils . . . held out to the people the most specious promises of assistance and protection." Some of the more influential men were traitors.

In 1261 the Icelanders, worn out by feuds and dissension, agreed to unite with Norway under King Haakon. The eastern province, which had been against this step, held out for a while, but adopted the same course two years later.

The oath of allegiance to Norway contained no startling departures from Icelandic thought. They agreed to pay taxes in the form of twenty yards of woolen cloth for every man who paid a parliamentary tax. The king promised peace and Icelandic law and in addition that six ships would sail from Norway to Iceland each summer. Land taxes were abolished. Inheritances falling to Icelanders were to be given them, and they were to have certain specified rights in Norway.

So far as the common people were concerned the union was in the nature of an improvement; for chieftains were forbidden to wage war on one another. The conviction that the government would maintain law and order gave a feeling of security.

Outwardly life went on as before, though with less truculence. But as Gjerset, himself a Norwegian, points out, the old vigor and originality were dwindling. Copyings and translations of old works took the place of creative thought.

The Icelanders, drawn into Scandinavia, were subject to the same decline. As with the rest of the Scandinavian peoples, no progress was made in trade or shipbuilding. The German Hanseatic merchants were gaining a strangle hold on commerce.

The hope of peace and security was not realized. Six years after the treaty which guaranteed the maintenance of Icelandic laws Magnus, King of Norway, engaged in fabricating a new code for his country, included the Icelanders in it. This code was brought to Iceland in 1271. It contained many provisions which were wholly unsuited to the country and omitted many provisions which the Icelanders considered important, for which reasons the people resisted its adoption, though vainly. Among other things it provided that officials of the crown of Norway should preside over the Althing, and that legislative powers should be exercised by the Althing and the king conjointly. Robbed of its national significance, the Althing soon lost its popularity and the general public ceased to attend its sessions.

In 1280 still another code was brought to Iceland. There was to be a sort of governor general. This and many other provisions created resentment. After discussion and dissension it was adopted by Althing in 1281, with the understanding that objectionable provisions would be revised.

As Gjerset sees it, the new code wrought "a fundamental change" in legal practice. "The king as ruler and lawgiver was regarded as the source of justice . . . Violation of the law was no longer viewed as a private affair to be settled by the offender and the party injured, but as a crime for which the wrong-doer had to answer to the government." However, the system of trial by jury of twelve men was retained.

Summing up the changes wrought in the first two decades of the union with Norway, Gjerset mentions the appointments of Norwegians as officials in Iceland, the bringing of defendants to Norway for trial, the reorganization of the Althing, and the introduction of Norwegian jurisprudence. Though some Icelanders still engaged in commerce their most important contacts were now through Norwegian ships and in the hands of Norwegian merchants who could not or would not supply the country's growing needs.

In 1299 Magnus, King of Norway, died. He was succeeded by his brother Haakon Magnusson. The Icelanders, mindful of the soft words and specious promises of the previous monarch, demanded that before they took oath of allegiance Haakon should redress their grievances. Their demands included the replacement of Norwegian with Icelandic officials, that Icelanders should not be taken to Norway for trial, and that certain provisions should be made with regard to commerce. Haakon replied that they were to take the oath of allegiance now and that the grievances were to be considered later.

In the following years this "consideration" manifested itself in the imposition of new and heavier taxes and, in effect, the relegation of Iceland to the status of a dependency.

In 1303 came still heavier taxes and the revoking of all privileges. The proclamation aroused a storm of resentment. The people refused to attend the Althing and set up local Things to take care of their own affairs. The king finally realized that it was impossible to collect the new taxes; so he quietly dropped the matter—without, however, doing anything else to redress Icelandic grievances. Interest in the Althing continued to decline; no assembly was held for about thirteen years.

In 1314 the king tried to right some of the grievances —for instance, he conceded that an Icelander should be taken to Norway for trial only if local courts were unable to settle the case. But he did nothing about appointing Icelandic officials and nothing about sending the promised six ships annually to Iceland, which had become more important than ever since trade was now a Norwegian monopoly.

The death of Haakon Magnusson left Norway without a direct male heir and the crown went to his three-year-old grandson Magnus Smek who was also the nearest heir to the vacant throne of Sweden. Norway and Sweden were thus united under one crown. When a Norwegian representative appeared before the Althing and asked the people to swear allegiance to the new king they refused and sent a memorial in which they reiterated their former demands and offered to take the oath when evidences of good will were apparent through a signed and sealed statement. That some effort was made toward conciliation is indicated by the fact that they accepted the king later that year.

In the beginning of the fourteenth century the Church exercised an oppressive influence. The bishops, now mainly foreigners, were interested only in the collection of revenues. Some of them made the tactical error of flaunting luxuries during a famine. By 1371 the resentment against them was so strong that Michael, Danish bishop of Skalholt, was driven from his bishopric, not to be replaced until 1394 when another Dane was appointed. Throughout the period Norway consistently supported the clergy and was herself interested in Iceland only as a source of revenue. Royal monopoly on trade continued; officials continued to be foreigners, without understanding of or sympathy with the people. Royal edicts were harshly enforced but general law and order were not maintained and crimes of violence were frequent.

Gjerset says of these centuries that "The jealousy and lack of patriotism of the chieftains . . . the selfishness and narrow-mindedness of the royal government . . . the greed and tyranny of the church had destroyed the people's public spirit and political interest, and had left them to wage their own struggles without the inspiring guidance of true leadership . . . A spirit of pessimistic unprogressive stoicism was fostered which was strengthened by the frequent recurrence of great calamities, and the sorrows, poverty and hopelessness which followed in their wake."

The fourteenth was a century of calamities. Cattle diseases, famines and epidemics had been their portion in the closing years of the past century but the new one opened with still greater horrors. In 1300 Hekla erupted and there were violent earthquakes. Farms were destroyed and fields were buried under a thick layer of ash. In 1301 and in 1306 there were deadly epidemics. In 1308 an earthquake in southern Iceland destroyed more of the farms and livestock. A further volcanic outburst in 1311 spread ash over wide areas, destroying meadows and pastures so that stock died of hunger and then the people. In 1339 an eruption in southern Iceland killed many and ruined many farms. In 1341 Hekla was active, destroying much grazing land. In 1360 the Mydal district was laid waste by ash so that cattle perished during the following winter. In 1389 the detonations of Hekla were heard over the entire island.

During the first half of this period Norway's world trade had declined under the competition of the Hanseatic League, but the Iceland monopoly was sustained. Some aid, however, was given to the distressed people. Many ships came and a fisheries export trade was developed. In 1349 the Black Death in Norway carried off about one third of the population, a blow from which she did not soon recover and one that weakened her maritime position, so that fewer ships came to Iceland. New taxes were imposed on Iceland's exports.

In 1397 the three kingdoms, Norway, Sweden and Denmark were formally brought together by an Act of Union. Eirik of Pomerania was the nominal sovereign; but the real power was in Queen Margaret who had been on the throne before the Act of Union and who continued to rule until her death in 1412. She was like her predecessors in that her sole interest in Iceland was revenue. She imposed still heavier burdens.

The Norwegians, as we have seen, showed little sympathetic interest in the Icelanders. The Danes cared even less. The Church continued in its greed. Violent resistance met the lay and ecclesiastical taxgatherers; the conflicts are recorded in the Icelandic *Annals*.

There were still a few people of some wealth in the country; but freeholders disappeared as a class, degenerated into peasantry. Schools fell into decay through the indifference of foreign bishops—but education nevertheless flourished. Individual clergymen throughout the country gave courses of instruction. Now the Icelander's love for reading stood culture in good stead, for it fostered home education and study, made possible a high standard of literacy. Gjerset considers that the Icelandic clergy of the period were better educated than those of Norway. He points out that although creative writing was at a low ebb some works of literary merit were produced. Copying, translation, and compilation occupied chief attention. "Iceland continued to be the center of literary life in the North."

In the fifteenth century literary activity was almost at a standstill. The Black Death ravaged the country in 1402–04 and by some estimates carried off two thirds of the nation. Many districts were almost depopulated. The people lived in misery and poverty, exploited alike by crown and church. Commercial relations with Scandinavia were only feebly maintained. Such contact as Iceland had was mostly with Britain.

The British had traded with Iceland during earlier centuries, but their commerce had ceased in the fourteenth. From the beginning of the fifteenth century it was resumed, over the protests of Eirik of Pomerania and, indeed, in spite of a formal prohibition decree by Henry V of England. Violence by English mariners against settlements and government officials in Iceland is recorded in the *Annals*.

The efforts of both Eirik and Henry VI to stop British-Icelandic trade resulted in the decrease of violence, but the trade itself continued. In 1450 Christian I of Oldenburg, who had succeeded Eirik, issued a decree by which English or Irish who traded with Iceland were to be considered as outlawed unless they carried his sealed permit. Their persons were to be seized and their goods confiscated. But Christian, like his predecessors, had little sympathy with Iceland. Involved in foreign wars and in dynastic problems, his only action, outside of the mentioned decree, was to order Björn Thorleifsson, the governor of Iceland, to resist the British as much as was possible. In his attempt to carry out instructions Björn was slain by angry British merchants who scorned a prohibition which Denmark was in no position to enforce. By 1463 this king seemingly had given up the struggle except that he forbade Icelanders to trade with foreign merchants who did not pay duty. Two years later he was able to conclude a treaty with Edward IV by which the English sovereign agreed to see to it that unlawful trade with Iceland be stopped.

The British merchants paid no more attention to these treaty promises of their sovereign than to the ones that had gone before. Not even the war between England and Denmark-Norway in 1469 was allowed to interfere in Iceland with "business as usual."

In 1490 a new treaty gave the British trading rights for a period of seven years.

In spite of the violence and the outrages which had characterized the early stages of British trade it was of the greatest possible importance to the Icelanders; for the British paid high prices, and paid them in goods which the Icelanders needed.

Beginning with 1430 the Germans also sent trading expeditions. Christian I, who needed their good will, granted them privilege of free trade.

The chief exports of the period were fish, sulphur, falcons, eiderdown, wool and woolen cloth, mutton, sheepskins, butter, tallow and oil. The chief imports were grain, flour, timber, iron, linen, pitch and tar.

Presently the Hanseatic merchants grew so powerful that Hans, who succeeded Christian I, sought to limit them by encouraging English and Holland trade. However, the Hollanders had no extensive relations with Iceland. Those with England were now declining.

In spite of the resented arrogance of some of the Roman Catholic bishops, the Reformation was not at first welcomed by the Icelanders. In 1537 Christian III had given his sanction to a new code which embraced the Lutheran creed. This was sent to Iceland, but no attention was paid to it. Stern measures were then applied. Gjerset says: "In 1541 the king appointed Christopher Huitfeldt governor, and dispatched him to Iceland with two warships. The mission of the governor was to secure the adoption of the new church code, to prevail on the people to take the oath of allegiance to Christian III, and to grant him a new tax . . . as he had been forced to carry on expensive wars to win the throne . . . The Althing of 1541 assembled under the drawn swords of foreign military forces."

Bloodshed and uprisings followed. The Reformation was not established until 1550 when Jon Arason, last Catholic bishop, and his son were beheaded at Skalholt. Church properties were confiscated and their revenues diverted to the royal purse.

During the sixteenth century relations were maintained with the Hanseatics and with Great Britain, some of the trade illicit but all of it to the benefit of the people. The attitude of Denmark to Iceland in that period is

Eiderdown has been an article of export for centuries. Farms with large nesting grounds are among the best properties in the country.

indicated by Gjerset who points out that in 1547 Christian III leased the country to the mayor of Copenhagen. His successor, Christian IV, in 1601, granted to the cities of Copenhagen, Malmö and Helsingör (Elsinore) an Icelandic trade monopoly.

What this sort of thing did to Iceland has been little appreciated by foreigners. Mackenzie, for instance, says that "The history of the island during the 17th century is almost wholly destitute of remarkable events." An Icelander may well find it hard to accept such an offhand statement on a period which influenced for the worse every phase of national life. The various edicts were designed to cut Iceland off from all intercourse with Europe, to restrict commercial relations to a few Danish traders. The results were tragic. No consideration was given to the needs of the people. To the crown an Icelander was merely a payer of a tax or in some other way a source of royal income. At one period trade concessions were simply handed over to the highest bidder.

The people had suffered under volcanic fire and ash, under famine and plague, but had survived. They survived the monopoly, but were weakened as never before. It lasted for 185 years, though in 1787 it was partially lifted—to the extent that the country's trade was open to any Danish subject.

We have mentioned rather than dwelt upon the role of the Church in the history of Iceland and might here add some points.

In 1607 a new church code was prepared for Iceland

by Norwegian churchmen through which the king's will became the highest authority in ecclesiastical affairs. Gjerset points out that the curtailment of the power of the clergy might have been beneficial, since some of the Roman bishops had abused it, but that the Reformation and the new ordinances "instituted a rule by royal officials who disregarded the Icelandic laws, acquired large landed estates, and riveted upon the people the tyranny of a selfish foreign bureaucracy."

Of positive benefit, however, was the reawakening of interest in education and literary activity in which the Lutherans had a share. The first printing press had been established at Holar by (Roman) Bishop Jon Arason in 1530. Little use was made of it in the early years of religious turmoil, but after 1572 it functioned energetically. Gjerset says that the literary works of the Icelanders were of high merit and that they attracted the attention of all Europe. Thormod Torfason published *Historia Rerum Norwegicarum* in 1711 and thus made available for the first time a history of Norway which could be read by scholars in all countries.

Perhaps, as Mackenzie has said, the events of the seventeenth century were not "remarkable" but that era saw many outbreaks of piracy when ships en route to Iceland were seized, when exposed coast settlements were ravaged. In 1614 Spanish buccaneers carried away sheep and cattle; English pirates robbed the homes of the Westman Islands on the southwest coast. Spanish and

English pirates appeared again in 1615, plundering, marauding. In 1616 Christian IV detailed war vessels to protect Icelandic trade. In 1618 he sent two royal commissioners with warships, attempting to drive pirates from the seas and to deal with church and state matters in Iceland. The attempt was not very successful, for in 1627 Algerian looters entered Grindavik, took a Danish merchant ship with its cargo and crew, decoyed and captured another ship outside the harbor, met armed resistance at Faxafloi, sailed to the Eastfjords where they seized cattle, took 110 prisoners and murdered others. In the same year they descended on the Westman Islands, drove the people into a storehouse, took the youngest and strongest prisoners and burned the rest. After destroying what they could not carry off, they returned to Africa and sold their captives as slaves. The survivors were ransomed in 1632; but of all those carried away only thirteen returned to their native land.

Wars on the European continent disrupted Iceland's trade; volcanic outbursts continued their untold damage at home. In 1618 and in 1619 much property was destroyed. In 1625 an eruption in eastern Iceland lasted for twelve days. In 1636 Hekla's fifteenth recorded performance lasted from May 8 until the following winter. In 1660 Katla's eruption destroyed large areas around Höfdabrekka. In 1693 Hekla broke out for the sixteenth time; ashes were carried as far as Scotland and Norway.

In 1662 by a coup d'état, Frederic III became absolute

hereditary monarch of Denmark and Norway. Iceland was asked to take the oath of allegiance simply as a matter of form, for refusal was impossible. The Danish monopoly was continued, though it was reorganized in the same year when a new company received a twenty-year charter. Iceland was divided into four commerical districts and by decree inter-district trade was forbidden. A few English fishing smacks managed some barter, but penalties were severe and no Icelander would attempt relations with a foreigner or with a native not of his district except in cases of desperate need. In 1684 new price schedules were established whereby Iceland's exports were reduced in price and her imports made costlier. Five years later the number of districts was increased so that trade became still more restricted. Gjerset cites many instances of severe punishments for infraction of the rules. Typical is that of a poor Icelander who was flogged in the presence of the Danish official because he had sold outside his district a few fish which the Danish traders inside the district had refused to buy.

The eighteenth century offered little encouragement to the hopes and ambitions of Iceland. The legislative power of the Althing had virtually disappeared; government was by a foreign power which cared little whether or not the welfare of the country was maintained.

Volcanic eruptions continued. In 1727 Oraefajökull began an eruption which lasted from August 3 until May 25 of the following year. Many farms were ruined and hundreds of sheep and cattle died. Earthquakes in 1732 added to the devastation. In 1755 Katla's ash covered a large part of Skaftafell district so deep that fifty farms had to be abandoned, while thirteen were outright destroyed. In 1783 Skaptarjökull's eruption laid waste large areas of meadowland; livestock perished, with resulting starvation of the people.

Throughout this century famine and disease further tended to break down morale. In 1707 a smallpox epidemic carried off 18,000, a third of the country's people. In 1757, 2500 died of hunger in the Skalholt diocese alone; it is estimated that in all more than 9000 perished that year of starvation and attendant diseases.

Poverty and wretchedness were everywhere apparent. Much of the land was now church and crown estates and the Icelanders were tenant farmers. No changes in rent were made from generation to generation, even though, in many cases, grazing lands disappeared under volcanic lava or ash. Sheep disease broke out in 1761 and in ten years reduced the number from 491,934 to 112,054, for which loss the tenant farmers were expected to pay. Houses were of sod and usually overcrowded, thus making for the greater spread of disease. Gjerset says: "How wretched and helpless the people must have been in such an environment, when smallpox epidemics and other dangerous diseases broke out, can readily be imagined. The sick and the well were huddled together in their dark hovels without medical aid, and usually even without proper food for the weak and suffering." Leprosy also descended on the country in this century.

A later chapter discusses modern Icelanders. Horrebow, a Dane, describes what the people of the eighteenth century were like:

The many ingenious Icelanders so eminent in the literary world, is a strong instance of their genius and good natural parts, and that they are not of a slavish abject disposition. Every year some of their select youth are sent to the university of Copenhagen, where they have constant opportunities of exhibiting their genius and capacity, which are discovered to be very remote from betraying an abject spirit, the reverse rather appearing in them, together with such a spirit of emulation for excelling others, that seldom or ever a dull person is remarked among them: and even in general the common people have keen cunning heads, and a deal of mother wit. As most other nations, they have a strong propensity to their native place, though one might think they would find more pleasure in other countries. . . . The Icelanders are also as industrious as most people in their several occupations, never neglecting or omitting any thing that ought to be done. . . . The general failing of the common people in most countries, proceeds from their being wedded to old customs, which they will not retract, unless upon the prospect of very comfortable advantage. This is the case of the Icelanders, though I presume, they are rather more cautious than obstinate, in rejecting their old customs; for I must confess, that I found them fond of seeing curiosities, and of improving themselves, as also very ready to imitate, very handy at making any thing, and very expert in turning things to advantage.

He speaks of the children who are "kept as tender, and are taken as much care of as the children of Denmark"; he tells of their education at home. He discusses the health of men and women. The women are as tenderly cared for as the children and are not strong. The men "are endowed with good bodily strength; but this strength continues only from the age of twenty to fifty, at which period it is usual with them to fall into a decay, by reason of the disorders that come upon them, and at last put an end to their lives." He blames this condition upon diseases and lack of adequate food and considers that doctors are necessary. He points out that in a country where occupational accidents are fairly frequent there should be surgeons to mend broken limbs.

Horrebow had been sent to Iceland in 1749 by the Danish government, for Frederick V had ascended the throne with seeming intent to better conditions. One of his needs was a comprehensive knowledge of natural resources; it was this survey that Horrebow was to make. He was recalled in 1751, however, and the work entrusted to Eggert Olafsson and Bjarni Palsson whose five-year survey was published in two large Danish language volumes—there are translations into several languages, one of them an English abridgment.

At this time there was bitter strife in Copenhagen between two factions of Icelandic students. One group, the Bishops' Sons Party, considered that Iceland's welfare would be promoted by "modernization," which essentially meant borrowing Danish customs. The other, the Farmers' Sons Party, believed their native land could best be served by preserving and developing the native culture. Other Icelanders joined neither side. The manœuvres of these factions must have confused the weak and vacillating Frederick. He did make grants for development; but his program had no lasting effect because he refused the one thing the Icelanders wanted most, an admission that they were a separate, non-Danish nation. Olafsson joined the native culture extremists. After his return to Iceland most of his writings followed this trend.

One of the Danish "developments" of this period was the construction of a prison. Mackenzie remarks that it was so much more comfortable than Icelandic dwellings that, except for the loss of liberty, an Icelander might well prefer to be in it. (This structure is such an important historical landmark that the Icelandic people have wanted to preserve it. With the building there, they used it; they are using it still. It now contains the offices of the prime minister and the other members of the cabinet!)

At least one suggestion of Horrebow's was acted upon. Bjarni Palsson, who had taken a medical degree in 1748, was appointed to the newly created position of surgeon general. Uno von Troil, reporting for the year 1772, says: "There is an apothecary's shop established on this island, and four hospitals for the poor and leprous, the care of which is committed to their most skilful physicians with proper assistants." This surely comes near drawing the long bow in the cause of pollyannaism.

The nineteenth century opened with small promise for Iceland. The legislative power of the Althing had ceased and there remained only a part of its judicial power. The Danish trade monopoly still had full sway and nothing of more than temporary value had been done to improve either the social or the economic condition of the people. The promising start made along the lines of health had come to nothing. Hooker reports for 1809:

"There are no hospitals throughout Iceland of any sort; that which formerly existed at Guvernaes having been dissolved, from being considered too burthensome an institution, and the poor wretches sent to their respective homes, where those deemed incurable are allowed a small pittance for their maintenance, which does not altogether exceed the sum of sixty-four rix-dollars per annum." (Hooker gives four English shillings as the value of a rix-dollar.) He points out that there are only six medical men in the country, most of them so far from their patients that they do little good. "The sick and the lame are seen crawling about in almost every part of the island, presenting the most pitiable objects of distress and misery. Nor is more care taken of the females, or of providing for the safety of the coming generation; as, though twenty midwives are provided by government, they are grossly ignorant."

Mackenzie the following year also reported six doctors. To the one in Reykjavik he gave a supply of vaccine which the doctor took thankfully as there had been none on the island for two years. He looked over the pharmaceutical laboratory and sums up that it was "well stored with old fashioned drugs of all sorts, most of them quite useless."

Mackenzie, obviously without being aware of what he is doing, gives an excellent picture of life in Iceland for the first decade of the nineteenth century. The attitude of the (Lutheran) Danes, for instance, is indicated in a paragraph which describes a Lutheran church service. "None of the Danish inhabitants appeared at this ceremony; nor is it customary with them to attend any of the religious services of the Icelandic church." Throughout his narrative, almost without exception, the well-fed, well-clothed, well-housed people he met were Danes.

Hooker, who visited the country in 1809, also gives a view of conditions. Discussing Reykjavik, he says that since it is principally inhabited by Danes it cannot be called an Icelandic town; "nor is there such a thing in the whole country; for, depending, as the natives must do, almost entirely upon the scanty produce of their own island, and requiring a considerable tract of country for the maintenance of a few half-starved sheep, such societies, as would form a town, or even a village, would be highly prejudicial and unnecessary."

As will appear in a later chapter, the Spanish Civil War of 1936–39 affected Iceland's economic life. So, too, in the early decades of the nineteenth century did the Napoleonic Wars cause distress, for they paralyzed sea trade and involved all the maritime neutral nations.

It is a common view that Denmark meant to side with England against Napoleon, and that it was a mistaken English belief which led to their shelling Copenhagen. However, the battle aligned the king with Napoleon, whereupon the whole Danish-Norwegian coast was blockaded.

The blockade was effective and suspended the Danish (monopoly) trade with Iceland. Gjerset relates that the Icelanders "made stirrups and horseshoes of horn, fishlines from rope, and buried their dead without coffins." Icelandic ships were seized by British privateers who raided the treasury and plundered homes. Under such conditions British trade with Iceland was revived, naturally against the protests of local Danish officials. Refusal of Iceland trade privileges to a British merchant vessel brought warships to back up the demands of the tradesman—so traffic went on. To that extent Iceland was gainer through the Battle of Copenhagen.

In these war years the trade of the United States with Iceland made a beginning. In 1809 the Neptune and Providence, commanded by Samuel Staples, brought a cargo of foodstuffs, brandy and tobacco. In 1810 another ship brought a cargo. In 1811 still another ship brought wares even better suited to the needs of the people—but on the return voyage it was captured by the English.

The war between the United States and England disrupted this first modern American commerce with Iceland, but in 1815 Edward Cruft of Boston, who had sent out the ships of 1810 and 1811, petitioned the Danish government to grant him sole American trading rights. These were granted on the recommendation of the Danish governor general, who testified that the goods were of value to the Icelanders and that the prices were low.

The "freedom of trade" which the British had established in 1809 was not precisely free, since they attempted to stifle all non-British competition. Moreover, trading became the more difficult through the financial collapse of Denmark and the consequent worthlessness of Danish paper money. Indeed even the foreign looters and privateers disdained it; they insisted on collecting their demands in coin.

In 1815 an effort was made to improve trade relations but Denmark did not take kindly to the idea. Through her alliance with France she had been defeated in the Napoleonic Wars and had lost Norway to Sweden. Her commerce was almost entirely gone and she set about salvaging what was left—a considerable part of which was the Iceland monopoly, over which she began to re-exercise control, starting with an order that British merchants already established should liquidate their holdings and leave the country.

However, although the policy was to attempt continuing the monopoly, it may be inferred that some improvement in conditions did take place since the population of Iceland began to grow, and herds increased. Cultivation of vegetables increased from 283 gardens in 1800 to 6749 in 1861. A setback to this development occurred through the ravages of sheep by disease in the years 1856–60. The number of sheep had increased to 516,-850 in 1853, but it declined to 326,664 in 1860.

Through difficult centuries the Icelanders had maintained continually that they were legally a separate na-

tion, not a province. Reduced to a status of economic
slavery without the means to better themselves while
shipping and commerce were in control of the Danes,
they carried on nevertheless the movement for liberty to
gradual success. Visitors of the period reported the people as "stoical" or "apathetic." A better adjective would
have been grim. Travelers say that dancing and games
were not much indulged in and that emphasis was placed
on the recital of the classic sagas. Mackenzie, for one, so
far underestimated the significance of this that he was
able to write: "The comparative eminence, however, to
which in this age (i.e., the saga period) they attained,
was not destined to be permanent; and the rapid ad-
vancement of other states towards civilization, con-
curred with changes in their own condition, to effect an
alteration in the balance subsisting between them" and
he goes on to discuss learnedly the decline, from which
he considered they would never recover.

What Mackenzie did not know, but what Gjerset, in
the light of evidence, appreciates, is that the old spirit
was not dead but slumbered, awaiting a leader. It found
leadership through Jon Sigurdsson.

After having been for some time no more than a
judicial body, the Althing was re-established as a legislative body in 1843. It was now held in Reykjavik and
had advisory legislative powers only.

In 1849 when the Danish absolute monarchy was
abolished Denmark conceded that Iceland should be consulted before final arrangements were made as to her

position within the realm. A national assembly was held
in 1851; but a motion in the Althing which would have
defined Iceland as a Danish province, with the right to
send delegates to the Danish parliament, was not passed.

The re-establishment of the Althing, even with its
limited powers, was a great concession from the Danish
point of view, but a futile sop to the Icelanders. Led by
Sigurdsson, they pressed on, concentrating first upon a
demand for the abolition of all restrictions on trade.
Their point of view was, naturally, regarded with less
than sympathy by the Danish concessionaires, who lob-
bied actively against it. On the other hand, the case presented by Sigurdsson and his followers appealed so
strongly to some in the Danish Rigsdag (where no Icelander had a voice) that they argued it was high time the
oppression of trade were ended. In 1854 this generously
democratic element became a majority, and on April 15
of that year Denmark passed a law whereby all nations
could trade with Iceland. As against the yearly ten,
twelve, sixteen, or no ships at all, the following year saw
125 ships coming to Iceland. Only thirteen of these were
non-Danish; but even so the traffic was profitable to the
Icelanders—for Iceland could now deal in a world market.

Sigurdsson actively campaigned for wider education.
He wanted agricultural schools and, as well, instruction
in medicine and jurisprudence. The government and
many Icelanders feared the expenses of such a program,
and it was postponed though its need was evident. By

1850 the number of doctors had increased only to seven from the six given by Mackenzie for 1810. This meant (for a country, remember, larger than Ireland) that but few of the sick could receive medical help. Law students were trained only in Denmark. No instruction was provided there in Icelandic law, so they returned to Iceland frequently with only a Danish point of view, an attitude which the government and traders naturally encouraged.

Sigurdsson did, however, live to see a beginning made in his educational campaign, for in 1876 a medical school, though at first with limited facilities, was founded in Reykjavik.

During this century nationalism was beginning to stir in Europe. Under the impetus of the French Revolution and the outcropping of free thought Germany began a systematic program for encouraging a love of the "Fatherland" and for eradicating foreign influence both in literature and in politics. From Germany the movement spread north to Denmark where it gained adherents through the poems of Oehlenschläger and the works of other young writers. In Iceland it flowered through the works of Bjarni Thorarensen and Jonas Hallgrimsson. Thorarensen wrote on national subjects. His *Eldgamla Isafold*, written when he was eighteen, became at once the national anthem. Of these two men, Kirkconnell says that they were the "Dioscuri of the poetic renaissance of the nineteenth century and each supplements the other in his qualities of spirit. Jonas Hallgrimsson is likewise important as a shaper of the modern literary language, purging it from excessive foreign borrowings, and moulding it into exquisite models of prose and verse."

Thorarensen concentrated on purification of the language and the revival of national spirit and tradition. Opposing him, a group headed by Magnus Stephensen stood for "being practical," the introduction of foreign words, with consequent enrichment of the old vocabulary. Clashes were frequent, but the side for which Thorarensen stood prevailed gradually. His rare powers of expression and insight had much to do with the reawakening of national feeling. Gjerset says of his poems that they were like "trumpet calls." While Thorarensen played upon the inner consciousness and appealed to honor, patriotism and freedom, Hallgrimsson dwelt upon externals. He extolled the countryside and appealed for appreciation of Iceland's charm.

These two men were followed by others. The movement to freedom gained fresh inspiration from activities in Europe and America where many old regimes had been swept aside. The American Revolution, the French Revolution, the Spanish constitution and the Norwegian constitution all had their effect in Iceland. The ground swell of world liberalization and the rise of gifted patriotic writers broke through the resignation with which the people had borne their oppression.

Fresh demands were now made upon Denmark for restoration of the power of Althing, for Icelandic law, for home rule. Various proposals and counter-proposals

The old and the new in Iceland. Pack horses bringing home the hay; a truck in the background.

were exchanged but none of the fundamentals were conceded. Once more Iceland was swayed by events in Europe where the liberal movement had reached its peak and, towards the middle of the century, had waned rapidly. In France the empire was restored, the Hungarian republic had been overthrown, the policies of Frederick William IV of Germany were frankly reactionary and the Prussian diet had been dissolved. Schleswig-Holstein's struggle for autonomy was regarded by Prussia and Russia as a rebellion against a legitimate ruler and Denmark was given a free hand to suppress it.

Denmark's main desire now was to solidify her possessions and restore unity. A convention originally called for 1850 to discuss Icelandic proposals was postponed for a year, to the disappointment and alarm of the people. However, on June 28, 1851, 140 delegates met at Thingvellir. The new constitution formulated by this assembly provided that the Althing would have legislative power in conjunction with the king. Denmark's reply was essentially that the Danish constitution should apply to Iceland *in toto*. Icelandic trade and budget questions were to be discussed and disposed of in the Rigsdag without even the formality of an opinion from the Althing.

But as the Icelanders continued to strive for their rights, every now and then some were restored to them. Freedom of the press was granted in 1855, four years after it had been established by law in Denmark. In 1859

the king agreed to sign texts of law in both Danish and
Icelandic. As already mentioned, the monopoly on trade
had been lifted.

In this period Denmark maintained that Iceland was
not economically independent, that her treasury showed
a constant deficit and that she could not therefore exist
without Danish support. But, as Gjerset points out, an
investigation plainly showed that large Icelandic revenues had been diverted to Denmark without return, and
that a fair adjustment would reverse the situation, making Denmark the debtor. Against the accusation that
Iceland did not bear her fair share of the burden of the
realm the country could show that Danish services consisted only of a few officials who were not wanted, and
that Denmark had never been able to protect the nation
from piracy, robbery or war.

An inquiry started through the efforts of Jon Sigurdsson led to the appointment of a joint committee of three
Danes and two Icelanders. There were majority and
minority reports as well as reports by unofficial committees and individuals. All agreed, even the Danes who
represented the Danish government, that Iceland had
been contributing (perforce) to the Danish treasury far
in excess of the value of support received from Denmark. All agreed that the financial situation could not
be cleared until the constitutional difficulties had been
solved.

In 1863 the king's message agreed to deliberate the
financial problem but neither the question of the consti-

tution nor that of finances was put before the Althing
of that year.

Once again affairs in Europe halted progress. In 1864
the armies of Prussia and Austria marched against Denmark. In that war she was defeated, Schleswig, Holstein
and Lauenburg were lost and with them Danish ambition
for a strong centralized monarchy. Their sole idea now
was to preserve what remained.

Between 1864 and 1869 Iceland's demands for solution
of the constitutional problem were pressed year after
year. The Danes still persisted in thinking of the country
as a dependency. In 1871 Iceland was defined as an
inalienable part of the Danish kingdom, but home rule
on purely domestic affairs was in some measure conceded. The Althing was not consulted about this bill
and received a copy of it only after it had passed the
Rigsdag. The new constitution, received at the same time,
was unsatisfactory.

In the summer of 1874 Iceland celebrated the thou-
sandth anniversary of her settlement. In honor of the
occasion the Danish king, Christian IX, and his entourage
arrived, bringing with them a new constitution.

Among those who attended the Icelandic millennial
were two Americans who later wrote books, Samuel
Kneeland and Bayard Taylor. Taylor was covering the
ceremonies for the New York *Tribune*, Kneeland was
on a pleasure jaunt. Both were keen observers, though
they differ on some points.

The king, as said, arrived with a new constitution and

a speech in which he expressed the hope that it would contribute to the prosperity of the people and the development of the island. Of the constitution, Taylor wrote (following a synopsis of its main provisions):

It will be sufficiently seen from this abstract how jealously the Royal prerogatives are guarded, and how carefully the Danish supremacy is provided for in a Government which professes to bestow a certain amount of autonomy upon Iceland. Yet, with all its illiberal and even despotic restrictions, the people accept the Constitution, for it is *something*.

Kneeland reports: "It is no exaggeration to say that the professions of power of self-government made in this 'new constitution' amount to little or nothing; as the royal prerogative opportunely steps in when there is any danger of additional liberty."

The effect of the king's visit on the Icelanders is reported differently by these authors, Taylor considering that he won friends and Kneeland that he created resentment, or that there was at best national indifference.

But let these Americans state their own views. Taylor says:

He [the king] has evidently taken especial pains to meet the shy, democratic Icelanders half way, and has been more successful than he probably suspects. The absence of the usual signs of profound respect among the people, often the stolidity of the man spoken to, the steady, unconscious stare of interest, so forgetful that his greeting is frequently not returned, must be quite a new experience for Christian IX. He cannot always quite conceal a fleeting expression of weariness or disappointment; yet I am sure that he is every hour making friends in Iceland. I have taken the trouble to ask as many of the people as can understand me, what they think of the King, and the one answer is: "He is very friendly, and we are sure he is honest."

Kneeland, reporting the same people in the same situation, writes:

Finally, my impression of this people . . . was that they are born republicans . . . The new constitution, though, in most respects, a "glittering generality," high-sounding words without practical concession of greater freedom, was accepted . . . as a beginning, the shadow of a substance in the future. Such concession on the part of Denmark alone can remove their national hatred . . . This, or at least a national indifference, was everywhere manifest during the recent visit of the king; the coldness of his reception was so evident that it must have wounded him, as, in his kindness of heart, he certainly wished to do something for the benefit of Iceland; he doubtless thought he had, but the keen scalpels of these republicans soon pierced the thin wordy covering of the long-drawn sentences, and came down to the hard skeleton of the old familiar despotism . . . The people looked upon the pageant, and said nothing; they even scorned, in their national pride, to use any language but the Icelandic, even when they understood Danish. There was little enthusiasm, except among the Danes, a few officials, and the aspiring demagogues who are found there, as elsewhere. . . .

As before, so after the document of 1874 Sigurdsson and his followers continued working toward a real constitution; but year after year drafts presented by the Althing were vetoed in Copenhagen.

When Sigurdsson died, in 1879, his able lieutenant Benedikt Sveinsson took command. Revisions were submitted to every session of the Althing till 1885, at which time the king replied that Iceland was inseparable from the Danish kingdom. But in the years that followed the struggle was renewed and to such effect that in 1903 Iceland was granted home rule.

To the Icelanders home rule, too, was but a step in the direction of making Denmark acknowledge that Iceland had never, legally and of her own will, belonged to any country. As Gjerset points out, the conflict which had raged so long was to the Icelanders one of principle. "In the light of such a theory the Icelanders could only view all bonds which united them with Denmark as fetters designed to keep them in a state of inferiority and subjugation."

In 1905 the dissolution of the Swedish-Norwegian union gave the Icelanders fresh grounds for courage and for activity. Finally in 1918 a joint commission of Danes and Icelanders was appointed to settle the relation between the two countries. Negotiations ended in the Danish-Icelandic Act of Union which recognizes that Iceland is an independent nation—in fact, recognizes the independence of each of these countries from the other so clearly that "Act of Union" is rather a misnomer.

The act, passed by the parliaments of both countries, declares that both are sovereign states; the king is called

King of Denmark and Iceland, or King of Iceland and Denmark, according to which people are speaking. For a limited number of years Denmark is to represent Iceland in international affairs. Equal rights are granted to Danes in Iceland and Icelanders in Denmark. The act further provides for abrogation. After December 31, 1940, the parliament of either country may demand a revision. If negotiations do not result in a new treaty within three years either parliament may abrogate the treaty.

Iceland is thus really free, after centuries of actual though protested foreign rule.

The 1940–43 outcome cannot at this time be predicted. Resentment against the Danes began to die down with the restoration of what Iceland considered her rights, and many are now in favor of continuing the "union." But there are many who want to cut even this slender thread, feeling that it does not affect national life in any practical, helpful way.

CHAPTER II

Literature

ICELANDIC LITERATURE is in some respects unique. It is almost as old as the nation by which it was created and covers a longer period than any other literature in a still living European tongue. The Old Norse in which it is recorded has in Iceland changed so little during a thousand years that any modern child can understand the old writings. For the children of Norway, and for Norwegian adults who are not students of the former speech of their people, it has to be translated—just as *Beowulf* and the writings of King Alfred must be translated for the Englishman of today.

By a comparative technique which he is fond of using Professor Ellsworth Huntington of Yale, geographer and historian of human cultures, brings out the per capita impression which Iceland has made upon the world. Since the achievements of the country are mainly in literature his presentation is a comparative statement on Iceland's literary position. In Huntington's view Iceland may almost claim that in proportion to its population it has contributed more to human progress than any other region except ancient Greece and Palestine. He reports that the Yale University Library, with no special interest, has 326 cards dealing with Iceland, while Ireland, with nearly forty-five times the population has only 1440 cards. Mexico, twenty times larger than Iceland, has 1200—only one fortieth as many as Iceland in proportion to population.

Discussing the number of men of eminence, he points out that Iceland's representation in the Encyclopaedia Britannica is proportionally higher than that of any other country but England and Scotland—towards both of which the Britannica had naturally a bias.

One of the criteria used by Huntington in judging the importance of countries is "the opinion of men of sound judgment." Lord Bryce, whom we have described in the Introduction, he considers to be the right sort of witness. Huntington quotes Bryce at length, among other things to the effect that of pre-Renaissance literatures the Icelandic is in quantity and quality second only to the classic Greek. Elsewhere he says the same thing by placing Icelandic literature between the Greek and the Roman.

Thomas Carlyle might also be considered the right sort of witness. In *Heroes and Hero Worship* he says of the classic Icelandic writings that they have "not graceful lightness, half sport, as in the Greek paganism; a certain homely truthfulness and rustic strength, a great rude sincerity discloses itself here."

The earliest kind of Icelandic literature is poetry. It had already made some progress in Norway by the time the settlers emigrated to Iceland; but in Iceland it later reached a high and peculiar stage of development.

Old Icelandic poetry falls under two heads: the Eddic lays and the Court poetry.

Most of the Eddic lays are of uncertain age, but it is generally supposed that much of what has been preserved dates from between 850 and 1050, and more particularly from the latter part of that period.

The Eddas are collections of lays and stories which tell of the Norse concepts of the world, of life, of the hereafter and of the fates of gods and men. They are two in number, the Poetic (or Elder) Edda, formerly but incorrectly believed to have been gathered together by Saemund Sigfusson in the latter part of the eleventh century, and the Prose (or Younger) Edda, written by Snorri Sturluson a hundred years later.

In spite of long and learned controversy it has never been definitely settled which of the lays were composed in Iceland and which may have originated in Norway or in the Norse colonies "West of the Main." In any case, they have been the exclusive property of the Icelanders as far back as written records go. Without them the people of England, and of middle and northern Europe, would have small knowledge of the religious beliefs of their forefathers. At least in clear-cut portraiture there would be no such gods as Thor or Odin, no Asgard, no Valhalla. Jacob Grimm might not have had material on which to base his law.[1] Wagner would have had scant material for his *Nibelungenlied*.

Good taste as well as good sense requires that testimony of this sort come from scholars who are not themselves Icelandic.

Sir George Webbe Dasent who, as we have seen in Chapter I, gives Iceland credit for instituting that trial by jury which was eventually taken up by England, is equally whole-hearted in giving Iceland credit as a preserver of knowledge:

Of that mythology, which may hold its own against any other the world has seen, all memory as a systematic whole has vanished from the mediaeval literature of Teutonic Europe . . . and, though . . . the skill and wisdom of the Grimms and their school have shown what power of restoration and reconstruction abides in intelligent scholarship and laborious research, even the genius of the great master of that school of criticism would have lost nine tenths of its power had not faithful Iceland preserved through the dark ages the two Eddas, which present to us, in features that cannot be mistaken, and in words which cannot die, the very form and fashion of that wondrous edifice of myth-

[1]"The correspondence of single consonants had been more or less clearly recognized by several of his [Grimm's] predecessors; but the one who came nearest to the discovery of the complete law was the Swede J. Ihre. . . . Rask, in his essay on the origin of the Icelandic language, gives the same comparisons, with a few additions. As Grimm in the preface to his first edition expressly mentions this essay of Rask, there is every probability that it gave the first impulse to his own investigations. . . . The importance of Grimm's generalization in the history of philology cannot be overestimated." Encyclopaedia Britannica, 14th edition, 1929.

ology which our forefathers in the dawn of time imagined to themselves as the temple at once of their gods and of the worship due to them from all mankind on this middle earth.

William Morris, in commenting on one segment of Icelandic literature suggests to the British that it should be to them what the tale of Troy was to the Greeks, and that it should be to all races what the tale of Troy is to all those peoples who are familiar with it in translation.

The present government of Germany, according to a dispatch in the New York *Times*, goes even farther than Morris. Part of its campaign for resuscitating "the fundamental and native religion of all true Germans" is to point out that not only must Germany substitute the Eddas for the Bible but that those Germans who formerly went to Palestine on religious pilgrimages (or those of like inclination) should now go to Iceland, "for Iceland is the Holy Land of our religion."

So Nazi Germany comes to the literature composed and preserved by the American republic of Iceland for the sources of her religion, as monarchistic Germany came formerly to the books of the same republic for inspiration and background of some of her greatest musical dramas.

The other type of early poetry, the court lays, praises the kings, especially for their munificence and valor. Occasionally they chide or offer advice. Sometimes a poet who had fallen into disfavor with a king would compose an encomium to save his head (*höfudlausn*, i.e., head-ransom). There are obituary lays, verses about the pagan

The bathing pool which Snorri Sturluson built in the thirteenth century—probably the first Icelandic domestic use of volcanic heat.

gods, about Christ and the saints; there are love ditties, humorous verses, satires, lampoons and dream songs. They reach their climax in descriptions of sea voyages; seafaring is a conspicuous theme. The poets used a great number of metaphors and synonyms. These sometimes make passages difficult to understand, but others are masterpieces of happy phrasing and deep thought.

When the court poetry ended, at the close of the thirteenth century, the poets composed *drápas* or lays on the heavenly court. The Virgin Mary, the Apostles, and other biblical characters figure largely. The most famous of these is the poem *Lilja* (The Lily) by the greatest poet of the fourteenth century, Brother Eysteinn Asgrimsson, a well-rounded work of a hundred stanzas, full of beauty and poetic inspiration. Translations are available in English, French, German and Latin.

In the latter part of the fourteenth century a new type of poetry, the *rímur*, was developed. They are based on mythical or heroic tales, on sagas or on European tales of chivalry and adventure. *Kennings*, circumlocutions, are used after the style of the old verse but are frequently unclear as to basic meaning.

The usual number of lines in a rimur stanza is four, but sometimes less. They end in rhyme, internal rhymes are sometimes found and they borrow alliteration from the court poetry. By varying the number and the length of the lines and by shifting the position of the rhyming syllables a great variety was obtained. Scholars have recorded as many as 2267 different meters. To such a length was this artificial rhyming carried that the poets composed whole sets of rimur in such a way that every stanza could be read backward and forward. Read either way the stanza was mechanically perfect in meter, alliteration and rhyme syllables; the meaning was in some cases approximately or exactly reversed, as in the case of our specimen:

> Grundar dóma, hvergi hann
> hallar rjettu máli;
> stundar sóma, aldrei ann
> örgu pretta táli.

Translated, this means: "His judgments are well-grounded, he never leans unfairly to one side of an issue; he cultivates honor, he never shares in deception and evil."

Repunctuated and reversed, the stanza has a reverse meaning:

> Táli pretta örgu ann,
> aldrei sóma stundar;
> máli rjettu hallar hann,
> hvergi dóma grundar.

Translation: "He leans toward vile deception, he never considers honor; he twists what is right to make it wrong, his judgments are ill-grounded."

There could be still further tricky ingenuity. For instance, if in the above stanza, first version, the commas in the first and third lines are placed after *hvergi* and *aldrei,* the stanza changes from praise to a libel—the effect is then about the same as that of the reversed stanza.

Danish ballads were introduced into Iceland in the fourteenth and fifteenth centuries, slipshod translations which enjoyed but a brief popularity. The same fate awaited the Lutheran hymns of foreign origin; they were recast, and native hymns replaced them. These developed gradually and reached their highest level in the Passion Hymns of the Rev. Hallgrimur Petursson (1614–1674). They are available in Latin and in English translation. Secular poems of the period began to take on a realistic tinge which continued into the eighteenth century.

In the nineteenth and twentieth centuries Iceland has produced many first-class poets who have in the main followed the old traditions, though with a wider range of subject and greater variety of form. Their poetry is on the whole intensely nationalist in spirit and, as has been discussed in Chapter I, some of them exerted great influence in uniting the people in a fight for independence.

Other types of poetry which developed were the funeral dirges, where the grieving poet recounts the life of his dear one and seeks to make his name imperishable. In this class are the "pony" poems. The pony is the most useful servant of the Icelander; and many a steed has had a funeral dirge a prince might envy.

Through the antiquity, through the individuality of the Icelandic poetic tradition, through the custom of intricate rhyme, meter and other devices, there are few groups of poetry more difficult to simulate in English than the lyrics of Iceland. Some of the more successful attempts are by Professor Watson Kirkconnell of the University of Manitoba in his *The North American Book of Icelandic Verse*, New York and Montreal, 1930, and by Professor Richard Beck in his *Icelandic Lyrics; Originals and Translations*, Reykjavik, 1930. Kirkconnell gives specimens of poetry from 800–1000 A.D. down to the works of living poets.

The most original literary achievements of the Icelanders are the sagas. Their material derives in some cases from remote centuries, their earliest written monuments from about 1100. The best of them had been transferred from the memories of the saga men to vellum manuscripts before 1300.

The saga had to be literature, for it could not survive unless it were popular. As between fact and fiction the word "saga" is noncommittal. It is cognate with German *sagen*, with English *to say*. A saga may be as factual as a Ph.D. thesis on the life and character of George Washington; it may be no truer than Weems on Washington; it need not even be that true. The sagas, indeed, run the whole gamut from books at least as truthful as their strongest rivals for that distinction of eight hundred or a thousand years ago, to yarns as nearly without foundations as a "western" of today. They might or might not be true. They had to be interesting.

The saga has many devotees, among them Hvaldan Koht, a professor of history and Minister of Foreign Affairs in the present (1939) Norwegian cabinet. One of his chief points is that most writings which have come down to us from the Middle Ages are "objects of study, not of enjoyment," but that the Icelandic sagas are living literature.

President Theodore Roosevelt once said that when he was tired and needed relaxation he fell back on the Icelandic saga (as President Wilson did upon the current detective stories). Roosevelt also brought up his children on the sagas, but that may be in line merely with parental desire to inveigle children into reading what they think good for them. However, the young Roosevelts liked this reading, as Theodore and Archibald at least have testified. The President's particular favorite was the *Njala*, but he enjoyed many others in their English renderings. The Njala translation he used was *The Story of Burnt Njal* by George Webbe Dasent, two volumes, Edinburgh, 1861. (Slightly abridged and without notes this text is available in many editions, among them Everyman's Library.)

So far as the sagas are concerned it was a mere coincidence that Bryce, whom we have cited earlier in praise of Icelandic literature, was Britain's ambassador to the United States during Theodore Roosevelt's presidency. For the Roosevelt children had been directed to the sagas by their father long before 1907, the first year of the Bryce ambassadorship. But that both men continued and shared their interest is indicated by Ilbert who says that: ". . . when Bryce was at Washington, President Roosevelt would draw up his knees and slap them with delight if he succeeded in eliciting Bryce's stores of knowledge about the Sagas."

A list of saga devotees would show illustrious names but it would make tedious reading. To increase at least the seeming likeliness that the foreign praise has foundation, we recapitulate who and what the Icelanders were at the time the sagas were composed and, later, while they were being transcribed on vellum.

Iceland was colonized by the strong Norwegian race; many of the settlers were "of high birth and independent spirit." They had seen much of other lands, were occupying an uninhabited country, were hampered with no laws but those which the natural conditions of the land, their own intellect, will and energy prescribed. In 930 they founded an aristocratic republic with institutions in many respects unique and their own.

The Icelanders had brought Norway's culture with them to their new home where it blossomed into a fresh, original growth. The old traditions were valued more than the gold and purple cloth which the sea rovers annually brought home with them to Iceland during those first centuries when buccaneering, the viking voyages, plundered Europe and northern Africa to and beyond the Hellespont.

The flowers of northern literature which bloomed in Iceland had at least some of their color from Ireland. We have mentioned the dispute on the percentage of Irish blood in Iceland, where the estimates range from a tenth to half. None will perhaps claim that half of Iceland's literature is from Irish roots. But neither will many grudge well more than a tenth of such credit as Iceland has from her literature to the people and culture of Ireland.

There is so much talk of Irish bards that it may be well to mention an average critical agreement that the poetry of Iceland shows less of Ireland's coloring than does Icelandic prose though some students credit the internal rhyme to the Irish and Watson Kirkconnell, for instance, considers due to Celtic influence "the uncanny horror of some of the Icelandic epics." The most factually historical of the sagas reveal least Celtic influence; it is the masterpieces of creative writing that show the most. The greatest of them in usual estimation, the Njala, is not merely in part Irish through its subject but has also seemed a work peculiarly indebted to the genius of the Irish people.

Many of the chief prose works of the twelfth and thirteenth centuries are family sagas. Family feeling was strong. The family was a kind of mutual insurance society; kinsman avenged kinsman or took *weregild* (blood money) for him. A man's position in the community depended largely on the offensive and defensive power of the family to which he belonged. The spirit of rivalry among the families made them keen to appreciate the characteristics and individual qualities of the various members.

Those were stirring times, particularly the tenth century when most of the events related in the local Icelandic sagas took place. There were quarrels, skirmishes, manslaughter and blood feuds, for the strong-willed and proud colonists were swift to avenge real or fancied slur or encroachment. Stories of these events were first told in the families involved; later they had a wider circulation. The Althing, as we have said, was more than a legislature. It was a source of news from all over the island and from abroad. So far did the Icelanders roam in those days that it does not seem strange that one of the poets has the line: *Lít ek um öxl til Krítar* (I look over my shoulder to Crete).

The eleventh and twelfth centuries are usually spoken of as peaceful, and they were in comparison with the ninth, tenth and thirteenth. Christianity was the official religion, following 1000, but the church was national in policy. In the latter half of the eleventh century we hear of men who are termed learned. They collected the traditions of the past, the genealogies and stories of events in bygone times, wrote them down and wove them into a more or less connected series.

The first matter that was reduced to writing was the old laws (1117–1118), and soon after that were penned genealogies which were to constitute one of the chief elements of the written saga, now about to take its rise. Ari Thorgilsson (1067–1148) was the first to write a history in the vernacular—the famous *Íslendingabók*, or *Book of Icelanders*. It covers the period from 874 to 1120 and has a scientifically historical approach. It became a pattern for all the later historians.

Ari's work opened the sluice gates for that historical writing which poured forth during the latter part of the twelfth and the whole of the thirteenth century in two main currents, one relating events which had occurred in Iceland, the other those from abroad.

In the great number of sagas grouped under the name of *Íslendinga sögur* (Icelandic Sagas), the action takes place in the tenth century and in the beginning of the eleventh. One, however, "The Story of the Banded Men," is an exception, for the events there related take place in the middle of the eleventh century. As the names ("Saga of Egil the Poet"; "Story of Burnt Njal"; "Story of Gisli the Outlaw") indicate, these are mostly individual and family biographies where the fortunes of the heroes and their friends and enemies are recorded. Some are more comprehensive and give not only the family's history but that of the district as well.

Serving as a test of reliability for the rest of the local sagas is the *Landnámabók* (Book of Settlers) which gives detailed account of the colonization, with the names of most if not all of those settlers who were looked upon as aristocrats, together with their genealogies and much historical matter besides. Then there are the *Thaettir*, short stories of the saga period, which are snapshots taken of Icelanders while abroad with kings or great men. These reveal magnanimity, firmness, sagacity and daring. They reflect both the history and the culture of the age.

A separate saga (*Kristni saga*) was written about the

introduction of Christianity in Iceland, and another (*Hungurvaka*) relates to the careers of the first five bishops who held the see of Skalholt. Hungurvaka and the Kristni saga are continued by separate sagas of some of the leading bishops, two of which date from the fourteenth century. "The Lives of the Bishops" are veritable mines of information; for about two thirds of the eleventh century they are our chief authorities for the civil history of the country.

From the first quarter of the twelfth century onwards, almost to the close of the thirteenth, we have on vellum a steadily increasing saga literature dealing with secular chiefs. These are preserved in the great composite work known as *Sturlúngasaga*. It was written by different authors but the main part of it is the work of Sturla Thordarson (1214–1284), Snorri Sturluson's nephew, and is called *Íslendingasaga*. It is the general history of Iceland during Sturla's own time, where special prominence is given to the author's own family, the Sturlungs. It is detailed and clearly incised description of Icelandic life and manners during this troubled period when the factions of the godar broke all bounds—a time of crisis, for it was to lead ultimately to the fall of the republic.

We turn now to the other branch of our historical literature. Ari, as we have said, was the first man who wrote in Icelandic a book on the kings of Norway. Others took up his work and at first narratives of individual kings, and of certain periods of history, appeared. Some of the authors of these sagas are known to us, as

Abbot Karl Jonsson, who put together the Sverrir's saga; others are unknown.

The most famous recension of the lives of the Norwegian kings and earls is that written by Snorri Sturluson (1178-1241) who put the coping stone, as it were, upon Icelandic historical literature. His immortal work, *Heimskringla*, is the history of the kings of Norway from the earliest times to the fall of Eysteinn in 1177. The introduction to *Heimskringla* contains the Ynglinga saga which deals in the main with Sweden. Snorri makes copious use of the writings of his predecessors, sometimes embodying whole passages from them. The work is polished. One thing prepares and leads up to another. His characters are drawn with understanding of every sort of man and motive.

Later, when Snorri's nephew, Sturla Thordarson, had written the sagas of King Haakon (*Hákon Hákonarson*) and his son, King Magnus the Law-mender, the Icelanders had placed in writing an unbroken record of the Norwegian kings from prehistoric times down to the year 1280. But they did not rest with this. They wrote of the colonization of Greenland and of life there; about the discovery of Vinland (the North American mainland) and the voyages thither; about the colonization of the Faroes and the quarrels of the islanders; about the Orkney earls and the colonization of those islands by the Norsemen down to 1170. They wrote a collection of stories of the kings of Denmark from Harold Bluetooth to the death of Knut the Saint in 1186.

At the close of the thirteenth century the Icelanders began to write down the *Fornaldarsögur Nordurlanda,* or sagas of olden times in Scandinavia. For centuries many of them had been handed down verbally from generation to generation. They were told for entertainment, and in them fact is so mixed with fiction that it is hard to separate them. Some are nearly pure fiction, where the hero possesses magic weapons, fights trolls and monsters and wins a glorious victory. These sagas are unlike the true Icelandic sagas in at least one essential: most of them have happy endings.

In the fourteenth century Icelandic manuscripts novels begin to predominate. Their heroes in some cases are known to have existed. Some were written in the style of the true saga, while others had the style of foreign chivalric romances.

Other branches of literature worthy of mention are the collection of laws (*Grágás*) from republican times; of the two codes (*Járnsída* and *Jónsbók*) which came from the union with Norway; of Snorri Sturluson's Edda which contains the Scandinavian ("Nordic") mythology, and *Skáldskaparmál,* a technical essay on scaldic versification. Four essays on linguistics also appeared, the first of which, about 1150, discusses phonetics and how the Latin alphabet should be adapted to the requirements of the Icelandic language. There were religious essays, and some on geography, natural history and mathematics.

The preservation of this literature, and the vital character of it, profoundly influenced the history of the nation. Because nearly every Icelander knew nearly every saga, and because every Icelander knew the favorite sagas, the rebel poets of the nineteenth century were not constrained, for instance, to speak of just "honor," an abstract concept susceptible of many interpretations, but were able to plead for a return to "the honor of Gunnar," a phrase with a precise meaning to every reader and listener.

Historical writing has never wholly died out. From the end of the thirteenth to well into the nineteenth century there is an unbroken succession of annals, of which there are now available some fifty or sixty collections, written by as many authors. It frequently happens that two or more annals cover the same period, whereupon they supplement each other. The mass of information is enormous. From them Professor Thorvaldur Thoroddsen has, for instance, compiled a book on weather conditions in Iceland during practically every year of a thousand years (900–1900).

Genealogy has gone hand in hand with history, so that most Icelanders can have their pedigree traced into the eighteenth century and many much farther back, some even to the first colonists of the country. There are people, for instance, with written genealogies extending to that Snorri who was born on the North American mainland (most probably in one of the present New England states or on the shores of the Gulf of St Lawrence) in 1004.

It is not possible to discuss Icelandic literature without speaking of the fairy tales. These deal with elves, trolls,

ghosts, magic, fairies, witches and ogres. During the nineteenth and twentieth centuries they have been collected
and several volumes have already been published. Mrs
A. W. Hall, who translated and edited one of the volumes, mentions a peculiarity—that whereas in most southern legends the heroic actions of the prince deliver the
princess, in many Icelandic tales it is the young princess
or peasant girl who undergoes the hardships and trials
and rescues the prince from a witch or giantess.

To discuss modern Icelandic writings in detail is beyond the scope of our present work. However, we speak
of trends.

In 1905 there fell to Cornell the library of Willard
Fiske who had been its professor of north European
languages and librarian from 1868 to 1883. There were
some 8600 volumes, pamphlets and articles. By Fiske's
will a fund was established for additions and maintenance.
The catalog of the Fiske collection, published in 1914,
consists of 755 quarto pages and lists works on all phases
of Icelandic life and thought whether by Icelanders in
their native language or in a foreign one, and by foreigners in many languages. In 1927 a 287-page supplement
appeared which covered additions to the collection from
1913 to 1926. Professor Halldor Hermannsson, Curator
of the Fiske Collection, comments on the later additions:

It will be sufficiently clear from the following pages that
the Icelandic presses have been very active during this recent
period. They have increased in number, and with them the
literary output.

He points out that many well-known writers have passed away and so occupy little space in the new catalog: yet others have come forward to take their places, and not a few of the new authors have already acquired some reputation, even outside the limits of their own country. Poetry still flourishes in the land of the old skalds, but it is now closely pressed in the race by novels and short stories . . . and even the drama, in a country without professional actors, is well represented. Foreign fiction has been translated at a rapid rate. . . . Religious writings, at least of the more orthodox kind, do not fill as much space as before, but new cults like spiritualism and theosophy seem to have many devotees, to judge from their publications. Books on music and musical compositions are also relatively numerous.

Especially noteworthy is the increase in scholarly works. It is clear that research, historical, linguistic and literary, has been greatly promoted by the establishment of the National University in 1911. The writing of text-books in the humanities and the sciences for lower as well as higher institutions of instruction is steadily advancing. . . . Further, the declaration of political independence in 1918 has been followed by an increased output of governmental publications. Besides the parliamentary and legal reports, noted in the earlier Catalogue, there are now various others, such as statistical, meteorological, and medical reports.

CHAPTER III

Iceland Today

THE ICELANDERS are of mixed Scandinavian and Irish descent, with other strains figuring little. One estimate has it that Norwegians, whether they came direct or by way of the British Isles, would account for 60% of the blood; that settlers from Ireland who had little or no recent Scandinavian admixture would be 30%; and that Scotland, England, Denmark and Sweden would account for the remaining 10%.

The debate on the Celtic element has been hot and at times emotional; so the estimates vary greatly. However, few if any scholars of standing place the Celts lower than 10% and only one has suggested their percentage may be as high as 50.

The racial, or more correctly national, elements have blended through a millennium into the Icelander of today. The census of 1930 shows the current non-Icelandic element to be only 1.3%, of which Danes are a third. This does not mean that foreigners are being discriminated against, legally or through being unpopular and finding residence in Iceland thereby unpleasant—though it may to a certain extent reflect the general wish to keep from permanent residence all non-Icelandic elements. Danes were about as loved by the Icelanders fifty years ago as the English were by the Irish of that time. But their decreasing interference with Icelandic affairs has increased the popularity of the Danes, till now there is scarcely a trace of the former bitterness. Icelanders are beginning to see why it is that modern Denmark is one of the best loved countries in the world.

It is dangerous to generalize about any nationality. Every country knows what it is to be amused or irked by sweeping characterizations of foreigners. What impression "the Icelanders" have made upon some visitors is indicated through the following quotations.

The Englishman, Lord Bryce, gives his impressions for 1872:

The average Icelander is more talkative than an average Briton, and much more so than a Spaniard; and though you would not call him downrightly gay, there is no want of cheerfulness and good humour. His position, "far amid the melancholy main," has not made him—as Mr Disraeli thinks it has made the Irishman—discontented with his country; on the contrary, he tells you it is the fairest land the sun shines on. . . . But there is a way in which external conditions do seem to have affected the modern Icelander . . . He is wanting in dash and vigour, and in the spirit of enterprise generally; has little promptitude in his decisions, still less in his movements. Nothing could be more unlike than he is in all these respects to those terrible ancestors of his in the tenth and eleventh centuries. . . .

Manners are simple in Iceland . . . and simpler . . . because there is really no distinction of rank. Nobody is rich, and hardly anybody abjectly poor; everybody has to work for himself, and works (except, to be sure a few storekeepers in Reykjavik and at one or two spots on the coast), with his own hands. Wealth would not raise a man much above his fellows, and there are indeed no means of employing it except in supplying a house with what would be thought in England indispensable comforts. Wealth, therefore, is not greatly coveted (although the Icelander likes a good bargain, especially in horseflesh), and an air of cheerful contentment reigns. The farm servant scarcely differs from the farmer, and probably, if a steady fellow, ends by marrying the farmer's daughter . . . There is no title of respect, save Herra to the bishop and Sira to a priest; not even such a title as Mr or Mrs or Esquire. . . .

As for society, it must not be imagined that there is any society in Iceland in the same sense as in England or America . . . There are no "county people," no "best sets," and hence no struggles to get into them.

The American, Russell, who wrote so glowingly of Icelandic scenery in 1914, says:

The people interest me. The country was settled not by serf nor servant. The grand old warriors of the viking period, who overran in quick succession the British Isles, ravaged the coast of France, swept through the Mediterranean . . . these are the men who, once lords and petty kings of ancient Norway . . . chose unknown dangers in

a strange and distant land. . . . From this virile race are the
modern Icelanders descended. They are a kindly, honest and
hospitable race; kind to each other and to the stranger
within their borders, hospitable with a hospitality which is
almost unknown in our selfish race, honest beyond all question.

The Swede, Lindroth, writing in 1937, gives the last
of our cited characterizations:

There have not been any momentous changes in the racial
material since the original colonization period, but in the
centuries that have followed, the Icelanders have certainly
had an ample opportunity to demonstrate that they constitute a happy mingling of races. They have struggled through
years of terrible distress, caused by a severe climate, volcanic eruptions, the Black Death, pestilence and famine.
They were sore oppressed by the Danish trade monopoly
. . . The people of Iceland have stood the test, often led by
men of indomitable energy who have had faith in the ability
of the people to win out. The Icelanders have always held
their heads high—or have raised them again after a fight.
They have preserved not only their excellent physical constitution, but their rich cultural heritage as well. . . . On
the other hand, a certain indifference in practical matters
has been noticeable down to our own day, and likewise a
lack of aggressive energy and precision. These limitations
are very natural in people who have seen how little man
can do against hostile external powers, the most inexorable
of which are the forces of nature. . . .

. . . We may say that the average Icelander is intellectual
in his approach. For that reason he remains a rationalist even

in religious matters, though we also meet individuals who
have a leaning toward mysticism. He has a well developed
self-esteem—even when he may have very little to be cocky
about—and is generally independent in thought and action.
. . . Freedom is what he values most, though in olden days
many had to learn what thralldom meant. . . . The Icelander does not like to subordinate himself in any way.
Nevertheless he must be called a democrat, for he is surrounded by none but equals, and has never had to take account of any marked class distinctions. In social life the
difference between rich and poor has never made that profound cleavage which in other countries has been the ac-
companiment of industrialization. We may well agree with
a German-Swiss authority on Iceland, Andreas Heusler,
who has characterized the Icelanders, somewhat para-
doxically, as "aristo-democrats." All these qualities have since
1918 had opportunity to develop more freely, and that is
what they have done, for better and for worse.

Discussing the reserve and taciturnity reported by
some travelers, Lindroth agrees that it does exist in
some individuals. "But it has been urged, and rightly,
that those who claim to have discovered this reserve are
often people who have not been able to converse with
the people in their own language. Moreover, it is nothing to people's discredit that they do not care to turn
themselves inside out before strangers. Where circumstances are favorable, there is plenty of good humor and
merry talk—though not more than in other places."

In these opinions of an American, an Englishman and
a Swede, we hope we have given a sketch towards a

*The Icelander is surrounded by none but equals; he does not
have to take account of any marked class distinctions.*

fairly accurate portrait of the average modern Icelander. What about modern Iceland?

Twenty years ago an Icelander could say with moderate accuracy that his country was for the traveler virgin territory. The tourist felt the thrill of discovery. Lord Bryce was correct when he said for 1872 that while a British traveler is in Iceland ". . . he may be offered a seat in the Cabinet, or accused of forgery, or portrayed in *Vanity Fair*—he will know nothing about it till his return." The strides in communication and transportation are changing all that. Through the radio Iceland, like every other country, is a listening post for the whole world's doings. The airplane which through winter and summer operation has shrunk home distances is about to make the country internationally a way station, a crossroad of transoceanic airways.

Not as recent in world history as the flying and the radio, but newer to most visitors than either of these, will be a use of a natural resource of which Iceland has a great store, indeed a store which she has often wished were not so great—volcanic heat. Because of the subterranean fires water rises to the surface at all temperatures from lukewarm to more than boiling.

When more than boiling this water has in the main a spectacular value, through the steam explosions that entertain residents and draw tourists. Of greatest practical value are the waters which do not explode, through being at temperatures just a little under boiling. Engineers have concluded that the best temperatures for the chief present use, that of heating dwellings and other buildings, is between 190° and 200° F. You can handle it in that range much more easily than when at boiling or over, for then you would have to contend with the pressures of steam.

The most convenient of the temperature ranges is found at the surface in some of the natural springs; it can be reached below the surface by artesian well technique in a good many parts of Iceland. In certain areas that are close to the 40,000 population center of Reykjavik and its suburbs you get within limited distances from each other places that have boiling water near the surface and others where you do not reach the 200° F. level until you bore down three quarters of a mile.

The first recorded use of Icelandic natural heat was near Reykholt in the thirteenth century when the historian Snorri Sturluson led water from a spring to a bathing pool which he had constructed near his house. (See photograph of Snorri's pool opposite p. 52.)

Apparently there was no utilization of natural heat from Snorri's time until the beginning of the present century when a farmer, again in the neighborhood of Reykholt, brought it into his house. Since then, as discussed in our chapter on agriculture, many farmers have used underground heat for many purposes—they pipe the hot water to their dwellings, to hothouses where they cultivate vegetables and flowers in every season, and to gardens where irrigation by warm water speeds the growth of vegetables.

In a dwelling the water has two main uses, to keep room temperatures at a desired level through radiating surfaces which warm the air, and to maintain at a convenient heat tanks of water for bathing or cooking. It is, of course, not the volcanic product itself that is used for cooking, but fresh water that has been heated through a coil in which flows the volcanic stream.

The first large-scale use was begun in 1929 at Reykjavik. Water was brought from near-by Thvottalaugar and used to heat the hospital, elementary school and thirty houses in the same neighborhood. Since then a number of other houses in the vicinity have received their heat from this system.

Plans are under way (1939) for heating the entire city of Reykjavik from the springs at Reykir, some distance away. During the last few years frequent borings have been made to determine the best place to tap the underground sources. According to the spot from which samples are taken, and according to depth of boring, the Reykir water varies in temperature from 190° to 200° F. It is estimated that on the way to the city there is a loss of from 4° to 6° F., so that you will have an effective pipe temperature in the buildings of 185° to 195° F.

To a country which has to import most of its fuel this program is of great economic significance.

With the introduction of modern improvements—electricity, radio, automobile, airplane—has come the inevitable change in mode of living. As in every country some of the passing generation regret that old customs are dying out. The youngsters welcome the change and the challenge. Nevertheless, the habits of thought and the manners that have endured for more than a thousand years change slowly. Many old customs may still be found. For instance, except insofar as a few have adopted foreign practice, patronymics are not used. A boy's "surname" is invariably the first name of his father with the word "son" added—thus a son of Olaf Jonsson whose first name is Sigurdur will have Sigurdur Olafsson for his full name; his grandson Jon would be Jon Sigurdsson. A girl's surname is the first name of her father with "daughter" added. Thus Olaf Jonsson's daughter Sigridur would be Sigridur Olafsdottir. Except when foreign custom is followed a girl does not change her name when she marries.

A foreign way of names, used by a few families, arose among those who either studied in Copenhagen or worked there. The surname, in these cases, was then usually derived from the home neighborhood as, for example, Blöndal from *Blöndu-dalur*, the valley (dale) of the river Blanda.

The introduction of "foreign" names was disliked by the home people. So in 1926 a measure was enacted which forbade the use of new family names. Those already existing might be continued.

The present form of government is a constitutional monarchy. Its constitution dates from 1920. Executive power rests with the King of Iceland, but he "exercises it through his ministers"; acts passed by the Althing "require" (and always get) his sanction before they become law.

The Althing is composed of forty-nine members, elected for a term of four years, of whom sixteen sit in the Upper and thirty-three in the Lower House. Of these forty-nine representatives, thirty-eight are returned by the twenty-seven constituencies as follows: one district elects six members by the proportional system; six districts elect two members each by direct vote, and the remaining twenty return one member each, also by direct vote. There is also a provision for supplementary seats, which may not exceed eleven, in order to secure a proportionate representation of the parties according to the number of votes cast for each at the general election; the seats can, however, be distributed only to parties which already have representatives in the Althing. All members receive traveling expenses and a fixed payment per day as long as the sessions last.

All Icelandic and Danish subjects have the right to vote at Icelandic elections (and Icelanders similarly in Denmark) provided they are twenty-one years of age, have resided in the country for five years immediately preceding the election, are capable of managing their own affairs, and have not been sentenced by a court for a "dishonorable" offense. All those who qualify for franchise are eligible for the Althing, except certain judges. The balloting is secret and takes place in every parish (*hreppur*) and town (*kaupstadur*). Absentee ballots are furnished to those who must be away from their districts on election day.

In the fashion in which the women of Wyoming were given the right to vote on territorial affairs in 1869 Icelandic women were granted the right to vote on local matters in 1882. They voted on clergymen of the State Church in 1886. In 1915 universal suffrage was secured to them, a newish idea then in world affairs.

The Althing assembles (usually in Reykjavik) for its ordinary sessions on February 15 or on the following weekday, unless the king has fixed a day earlier in the year. The king summons the Althing and decides when it shall be prorogued, which, however, must not be done until the budget has been passed. He may summon extraordinary Althings. He may also adjourn its meetings once a year for a certain period of time. Without the sanction of the Althing this must not exceed two weeks. He has the right to dissolve parliament, but if this is done a new election must take place within two months, and the new Althing must be summoned not later than eight months after the previous parliament was dissolved.

Although the Althing is in the main a legislative assembly it can both control and influence the administrative work of the government because it commands the sources of supply. Both the budget proper and the supplementary budget require its sanction. No payments can be made from the public treasury unless authorized by the Althing. Its sanction is required for imposing, changing, or abolishing taxes, duties and customs; for the state's taking up loans; for the uses to which public domains are put. It appoints a board of three auditors to examine the national accounts of revenue and expenditure during each financial year. Through its addresses to the king and resolutions and questions to the government the Althing has a further control on public affairs.

The Ministry of Justice and Ecclesiastical Affairs includes: civil and criminal administration of justice, police, prisons, matters relating to family rights, inheritances, rights of property, ecclesiastical affairs, public health, education (except agricultural schools), elections to the Althing and publication of the official *Gazette*.

The Ministry of Industry and Commerce has charge of all matters relating to industries, communications (postal, telephone and telegraph), municipal affairs and the public domain.

The Ministry of Finance supervises the country's financial affairs in general, taxes, customs, administrative auditing, banking and the registration of vessels.

Locally the work of government is carried out by district or town magistrates with the co-operation of district or town councils.

Issues were not very clean-cut between political parties in Iceland up to 1918, when the country achieved its independence. Before that time party division was mainly on the *degree* of independence, the Home Rule party and the Independence party standing for the things signified by their names. These two were the chief parties in the Althing during the second decade of the present century, although minor parties were beginning to develop. Thus in 1916 some agrarian members of the Althing formed what was to be the forerunner of the Progressive party, whose platform called for promotion of co-operatives and of agricultural interests. In the same year the Labor party was formed by the working classes. In 1924 the Conservative party was formed mainly from what was left of the home rulers, while the Independence party continued as such until 1926 when it changed its name to Liberal. In 1929 the Conservatives and Liberals joined forces and became the Independent party, with a platform calling for political and financial independence of the country, free trade and individual initiative. They are the chief opponents of the Labor party and derive their support from the commercial classes, employers and from a certain number of rural supporters.

In 1930 the left wing of the Labor party branched off and formed the Communist party, affiliating themselves with the Third International in Moscow.

With all these parties, recent governments have usually been coalition. Of the last three two were coalitions where the Progressives each time had two of the Cabinet memberships and Labor one. In the present government Labor has supported the Progressives to the extent that they helped them to carry parliament; but through lack of sympathy with what they consider an important issue they have withdrawn their member from the Cabinet so that the present (1939) Cabinet is entirely from the Progressive party.

To state the 1939 situation for Althing: The strongest party (Progressives) favors co-operatives; the second strongest (Independents) favors private capitalism; the third strongest (Labor) wants government ownership; and the weakest, with four members, is the Communist party. There is a party modeled along Nazi lines, but they have not been able to muster enough votes to elect a member to Althing.

The majority of Icelandic newspapers represent different shades of political opinion and can therefore be grouped according to political parties. Papers supporting the Independent party are: *Morgunbladid* and *Vísir* (dailies), *Isafold og Vördur and Stormur* (weeklies), all published in Reykjavik, *Íslendingur* (weekly) published in Akureyri, *Vesturland* (weekly, Isafjördur), *Siglufirdíngur* (weekly, Siglufjördur), and *Vídir* (weekly, Vestmannaeyjar). Papers supporting the Progressive party are: *Timinn* (three times a week) in Reykjavik, *Dagur* (weekly, Akureyri), *Einherji* (weekly, Siglufjördur). Labor or Socialist papers are: *Althydubladid* (a daily with a weekly edition, Reykjavik), *Althydumadurinn* (weekly, Akureyri), *Skulfull* (weekly, Isafjördur). The Communist party has two papers, *Thjódviljinn* (daily, Reykjavik) and *Verkamadurinn* (issued twice a week, Akureyri). The Agrarian or Conservative Farmer party issues a weekly paper, *Framsókn* (Reykjavik).

The rights of citizens as guaranteed by the constitution provide for free speech, free press, free assembly and freedom of religion. For although the Lutheran Church is the established church, no one forfeits civil rights for his religious opinions. It guarantees industrial liberty and provides parish relief for the destitute; it forbids unlawful arrests, deprivation of property, the enactment of laws conferring exclusive privileges of nobility, title or rank. It defines regulations that may apply to foreigners. Under it defense of the country is obligatory on every man able to carry arms, according to a system which may later be fixed by law.

However, Iceland has no military force and has declared herself permanently neutral.

CHAPTER IV

Education

THE FIRST SCHOOLS of Iceland were founded in the eleventh and twelfth centuries and were mainly religious in character, although some of them taught other subjects as well. These schools began to suffer a decline in the thirteenth century. From that time until the revival of formal education in the fifteenth, the old saga literature, the Althing traditions and the Jonsbok (code of laws) served as textbooks in the homes of the common people and maintained a continuance of literacy. Many Icelanders could read and write when those arts were unknown to similar groups in Europe.

In 1810 when Mackenzie was in the country there was only one school, a boarding academy at Bessustad with three masters and twenty-four pupils. In 1863 the same was reported by Baring-Gould, though the number of students had risen to about forty. The high degree of literacy continued to be maintained by home instruction, where son and daughter were alike taught by father or mother, with instruction in Latin and Danish provided by the local clergyman. This type of Latin instruction explains what many travelers have reported: that Icelanders spoke Latin to foreigners who did not understand their native tongue.

In 1834, for example, alongside of his descriptions of the miserable poverty, John Barrow, Jr, reports: "One thing, however, is certain: not only the clergy of Iceland, but numbers of the peasantry are well versed in the classics, particularly in Latin, which they write with fluency."

The Rev. P. C. Headley says for the year 1874:

"We may have one of the pleasant surprises common to tourists in Iceland, if we call upon the weather-beaten fisherman, Zoega, whose little boat rocks upon the waves, while he drops his line for hours together . . . to secure a scanty supply of food for his lava-sheltered family. We cannot speak Icelandic; so Zoega tries the purest Latin: if he fails here, he may resort to Greek, certainly to Danish, or some other modern tongue. Or pause before that smithy, where another plain, poor man hammers out . . . his livelihood. His salutation is in elegant Latin."

Bayard Taylor reports for the same year, that when his seventeen-year-old guide was puzzled by an English word he would ask, "What is it in Latin?" The boy also spoke a reasonably fluent German. The range of his interest was so wide that it startled Taylor who remarked: "And this was a poor, fatherless boy of seventeen, with only an Icelandic education!"

It has been contended plausibly that the farmer Latin

vocabulary of Iceland was in reality small and bad. For one thing, the traveler who enthused over it may not have been a good enough Latinist himself to render sound judgment; for another, he would have been so startled on finding any Latin at all that he went into ecstasies where no more was really justified than condescending praise. We have this expressed, for instance, by C. P. Ilbert who writes an "Appendix to Chapter on Iceland" for Bryce's *Memories of Travel*. He calls priests those whom others call farmers—both designations being likely enough correct, since a country minister would be a farmer too. Ilbert says that "The up-country priest would occasionally produce a Latin sentence or two, though the up-country Latin was apt to be queer."

However, some of the derogatory traveler opinions of the wayside Latin of Iceland can have been due to the pronunciation. Besides, you may read a language fairly well though you are not able to speak it at all, particularly if you are self-taught. Nowadays a traveler in Iceland who speaks in English to a farmer may get no adequate reply and still receive an appropriate answer to the same words if he were to write them in a clear hand and take the reply also in writing.

It was a hundred years ago that Barrow found a "number of the peasantry" writing fluent Latin and for that same year he reported that the clergy could refuse to perform marriage services for a woman who did not know how to read and write. The observations of Headley, Taylor and Bryce were more than sixty years ago.

During those sixty years home education has been replaced by school education, and thereby have developed
in Iceland those group distinctions between the schooled
and the unschooled with which we are familiar from
nearly every land. The establishment of numerous
schools following 1900, and the more widespread teaching of one or more current foreign languages, is now
throwing conversational Latin and Greek into the dis-
card. But you still find some remnants of them, particularly Latin, in out-of-the-way places.

A significant force in popular education through the
schoolless centuries, a characteristic of Icelandic life, had
been the *Kvöldvökur* (Evening Wakes) where one person read aloud from the sagas, or recited rimur lays,
while the others worked at quiet indoor tasks. The
Kvöldvökur usually began in the afternoon, with the
start of the early winter twilight, and continued until
bedtime; they were held only in winter when most outdoor work was impossible. In the tenth to fifteenth centuries professional bards went from farm to farm, but
later some one person in the family group was selected
to do the reading, particularly from the seventeenth century when printing was introduced and the vellum and
other manuscripts and storehouses of memory no longer
had to be drawn upon exclusively. The Kvöldvökur, the
saying of family prayers, the reading aloud from religious books, survived down into the second decade of
the twentieth century. Changed occupational life, in-

creased mechanization and the radio are now bringing these old customs into disuse.

The new conditions presented Iceland with a new educational problem. Parents were no longer able or willing to instruct children at home as they themselves had been instructed. An elementary school system therefore had to be developed and now must deal with three main groups of children, large concentrations in the cities, smaller groups in the towns and children living on isolated farms.

The cities and towns now have satisfactory day schools; but the problem of educating the country children is not yet mastered. Wherever possible, boarding schools have been set up to accommodate those children who cannot reach schools from their homes daily, but this building program is not yet far advanced.

Once a chief agency of compulsory education, the movable school still continues in rural districts, though with signs that it may soon disappear. Under this system children do not meet at a special building but gather at one of the larger farms in the district. There they stay for a few weeks and move on to another large farm, the teacher moving with them.

While education is compulsory the age limit and the amount of instruction vary with the type of school. City schools require attendance between the ages of seven and fourteen; their school year is nine to nine and a half months. This applies to all the larger town schools as well. In other day schools children under ten receive 500 hours instruction, older ones 600 hours; the school year is from six to seven months. Boarding school children receive a minimum of sixteen weeks of instruction a year, and attendance is compulsory between the ages of ten and fourteen. The "movable school" year is six months, and each child receives a minimum of twelve weeks instruction. In all the public schools tuition is free.

Private schools are permitted, but they must conform to standards set by the Ministry of Education. They are not, of course, given a state subsidy.

In Reykjavik there are special schools—for the deaf and dumb, the blind and for mental defectives.

Compulsory education ends with the elementary schools. Passing the final examination enables a child to go on to a continuation school. Most of the towns have high schools, with two- or three-year courses and seven-month terms. In rural communities there is the folk school which offers courses for two-year periods of six months each. Their object is to prepare students for work under Icelandic conditions of life through books and through manual and physical training.

Cities and the larger villages also have night schools. Common subjects in these are Icelandic, arithmetic, physics, chemistry, bookkeeping and at least one foreign language. The schoolwork is based on the trades pursued by the various students, and field work is done in the service of the trade or craft concerned. These schools enjoy a subsidy from public funds but the enterprises to which students are apprenticed pay school fees. Among

Healthy, happy children are a country's chief asset.

the occupations for which training is given are bakers, motor mechanics, tinkers, bookbinders, brush makers, gas fitters, goldsmiths, boilermakers, tailors, milliners, confectioners, cablemen, printers, masons, electricians, barbers, radio mechanics and paper hangers. There are many more.

The period of apprenticeship is three to four and a half years. When this time has been served, and an examination passed, the apprentices get a journeyman's ticket in their trade or craft. The annual session of the Reykjavik Technical School is eight months; those of the other schools four to six months.

In addition to these evening schools a kind of "work school" is held in Reykjavik and in some other places. The courses given are about the same as in the folk schools—Icelandic, arithmetic, manual and physical training—and they are intended for young people who are out of work or who for one reason or another do not attend other schools.

There are two college preparatory schools in Iceland, one in Akureyri, the other in Reykjavik. These schools are free, but entrance is by competitive examination. Graduation brings with it the right to enter the university.

Down to the year 1876 higher education was available only along religious lines for the pupils of the Latin School (grammar school); the Theological Seminary offered courses that prepared students only for ordination to the ministry. In Chapter I we have discussed the eagerness of Jon Sigurdsson for the establishment of schools of law and of medicine, for training in either profession was at that time available only through taking the course in Copenhagen. Sigurdsson lived to see a medical college established in Reykjavik in 1876. The law school was founded in 1908. On June 17, 1911, the hundredth anniversary of Sigurdsson's birth, these three branches were united into one, the University of Iceland.

The University has five faculties: Theology, Medicine, Law, Philosophy and Research. Two of these names require an explanation: Philosophy is defined as representing Icelandic philology and history; Research covers three departments which work for the benefit of the fisheries, industry and agriculture.

The University is a coeducational state institution. Its chancellor is elected by the teaching staff from among their number for a term of three years, and he is supported by the Academical Consistory which is composed of the deans of the faculties. Lindroth says of the University staff: "The professorial chairs are still few in number, but several of them are occupied by really eminent men."

Several European countries have sent the University exchange professors to lecture on their languages or their literature and sometimes on other subjects. Iceland in like manner sends scholars abroad upon invitation, more frequently to European centers but also to America. An example is that through the academic year 1931–32 Sigurdur Nordal, professor of Icelandic literature, lectured in Harvard University as Charles Eliot Norton, Professor of Poetry.

The University was homeless when it was first organized and it had to be temporarily housed in the parliamentary building. Money for construction of its own house was raised through a national lottery begun in 1933 and continuing until 1943. After 1943 lottery funds will be used also to finance other public buildings.

Because of the limited number of subjects taught in the University many continue their studies abroad. The choice of university depends on where it seems they can get the best education in their particular subjects, and special grants are made in the national budget each year to send approved students to schools thought best for them.

In addition to the schools we have mentioned there are a variety of special institutions—commercial schools, navigation, engineering, agricultural, horticultural, music-teachers' training, domestic science and the like.

The control of all schools rests with the Minister of Education. Under him a director sees that laws and regulations are observed and gathers statistics and other information. School committees in every district superintend and inspect individual schools.

The development of schools has long been a political bone of contention for, like some other countries, Iceland is now coping with a surplus of students. One group wants certain restrictions for the higher schools such as entrance examinations, for instance. Their opponents feel the schools should be for anyone who cares to use them. The University faculty and its student body are on the side of unhampered education. These debates occupy much space in the newspapers around election time.

Meanwhile the educational system is being steadily improved. Many teachers have gone abroad to secure acquaintance with the newest ideas and methods. The largest single group are those who visit one or another of the Scandinavian countries; but many have studied in Great Britain, Germany, France, Switzerland and the United States. Most teachers in the preparatory schools and in several other secondary schools have done graduate study in foreign lands.

Thus many foreign ideas have been introduced into the Icelandic system of education, some of them intact and others changed to meet local needs. The thought behind is to serve and strengthen everything good that is native to the country while keeping in step also with the march of world progress.

Aside from formal education there are many societies for the promotion of science and culture.

The Union Fund (*Sáttmálasjódur*) initiates and encourages scientific research; supports the publication of learned works and of textbooks for the University; grants pecuniary aid to laboratories, museums and the University library; gives awards to Icelanders who produce scientific works deemed worthy; grants traveling funds to professors and university graduates to enable them to go abroad for research and study.

The Fund for the Promotion of Culture (*Menningarsjódur*) was created in 1928 to promote general culture and national art and to further the study of Icelandic natural history. This fund is derived from fines paid for violations of the liquor law and also receives a share of the profits made by the State Liquor Monopoly. One third of its income is used for the publication of a popular science series and standard works of fiction both native and foreign; one third supports the study of nature and publication of works dealing with natural history; the remaining third purchases works of art for the art collection and gives prizes to those who publish architectural designs and designs for furniture or who offer patterns for home industries on national lines. This fund is administered by a council of five elected by the Althing for a period of four years. Menningarsjódur carries out all transactions with regard to works of art and supervises distribution of the art budget and of scholarships to Icelandic students at foreign universities.

The Icelandic State Broadcasting Service was opened at Reykjavik in 1930. It is owned and operated by the state, deriving its revenue from a tax on receiving sets. The broadcasting service is managed by a government-appointed director, but the program is arranged by a committee of seven members who are elected for four-year terms. The chairman is appointed by the Cabinet, while the Althing and the radio listeners each appoint three of the other members.

There are several other societies which work for the

diffusion of science and general culture. They enjoy a subsidy but are mainly dependent upon subscriptions. Subscription rates are low; the number of subscribers is very high in proportion to the population.

The oldest of these societies is the Icelandic Literary Society (*Hid íslenzka Bókmenntafélag*), founded in 1816. Besides an annual containing short articles it publishes scientific and learned works, chiefly dealing with Icelandic history and literature. The Society of Friends of the Icelandic People (*Hid íslenzka Thjódvinafélag*), founded in 1869, was originally political but soon began to issue a popular science series. It also publishes two annuals.

The Icelandic Archaeological Society (*Hid íslenzka Fornleifafélag*), founded in 1879 for the collection and preservation of antiquities, issues a yearbook on archaeological matters. Of it Lindroth says: "In more recent times there has been a systematized effort to dig out of the ground the relics of bygone days. The sagas furnish full information about the appearance and arrangement of the heathen sanctuaries; and this has been supplemented in a most valuable way by the archaeological investigations on the old temple sites."

The Icelandic Natural History Society (*Hid íslenzka Nátturufraedisfélag*), founded in 1889 for study and for collecting natural history specimens, publishes an annual report. The Icelandic Historical Society (*Sögufélagid*), 1902, publishes texts dealing with the history of Iceland from about 1500 onwards. The Early Icelandic

Text Society (*Fornritafélag Íslands*) was founded in 1928 to bring out a standard edition of the old Icelandic classics, complete in thirty-five volumes. Several have already appeared.

Among societies of a more exclusive character are the University Men's Union, founded 1871; Iceland's Scientific Society, founded 1918 by professors and other men of science; the Icelandic Medical Society, the Teachers' Association, the Association of Icelandic Clergymen, the Association of Civil Engineers. All these have their own publications.

In the interests of physical culture a number of athletic clubs and unions have been organized. Wrestling (*glíma*) in Iceland is fundamentally different from the Greco-Roman style, depending rather on suppleness than on weight or strength. Lindroth says of it:

"First we must mention the sport which even to the foreigner stands out as something particularly characteristic of Iceland, namely, that form of wrestling known as the *glíma*. . . . Here there is no classification . . . into heavyweights, featherweights, and so forth. But there are plenty of rules, and a far greater number of tricks." After describing the position which the opponents must take and the object which is, of course, for one to throw the other, he continues: "This is done by quick movements, most of them with the feet, but also with the hands, and these rapid turns constitute the tricks." He mentions that twenty-two tricks are known by special names.

The glíma is a part of every athletic program given in the country.

Next in popularity is swimming. This is facilitated by the ease of securing warm water for the swimming pools from hot springs. The first society for regular instruction was founded in 1884.

On the south coast skating of consequence is a recent development—the ponds in southern Iceland do not often remain frozen long enough for young people to learn. However, Reykjavik now has a skating rink. In the north of Iceland skating has long been a popular sport.

Skiing has been practised in all those parts of Iceland where the cold spells of winter are fairly long, but only during the last few years have ski clubs been organized. Experts have been brought in from other countries as instructors. It is a far cry from the early days, when skis were something used after a heavy snowfall when you wanted to get from one place to another, to the present generation who look upon it chiefly as a sport. Right near the city of Reykjavik there is seldom snow for skiing; but suitable fields may be reached by an automobile ride. A ski clubhouse now stands some twenty miles inland from Reykjavik.

Other sports practised are football and various other types of ball playing. Glider flying has become popular the last few years and gliding clubs are being organized.

All athletic clubs and unions are under the control of the Icelandic Sports Union, founded 1912.

In addition to the publications of the described societies

and associations there are many monthly and quarterly periodicals, some literary and general, others devoted to special trades or professions.

We have mentioned the Icelander's love for books. In consequence there are more publishers who put out general and special books than would be looked for in a country of 120,000 people. One estimate has it that Icelanders read per capita seven times as many books and serious journals (including art and literary magazines) as the next most "literate" country. Even if that be not so, the statement is true in implication, at least to the extent of meaning that reading is a passion with the Icelanders.

There are five daily papers, thirteen weekly and one which is issued twice a week. These represent the views of the various political parties and are described in the chapter "Iceland Today."

Also contributing to education are the libraries. The National Library, founded in 1818, is the largest in the country. It contains some 138,000 printed books and about 8500 manuscripts. Its collection of books on chess, among the largest of its kind in the world, was bequeathed by the late Professor Willard Fiske of Cornell (author of the book *Chess in Iceland*, Florence, 1905). The library receives free two copies of every publication printed in Iceland. Other Reykjavik library collections are those of the Mentaskoli, the Althing, and the Public Library.

Outside the capital there are four regional libraries,

one for each quarter of the land. They are entitled to one
free copy of each publication (of two sheets and over)
printed in Iceland. Almost every district has its public
library, and circulating libraries are to be found in the
parishes, some of them having considerable collections
of books.

The Collection of Icelandic Antiquities, founded in
1863, is now the Icelandic National Museum, which may
pre-empt all Icelandic relics that are discovered. The
curator has as well the care of all remains and ruins,
wherever found in the country. Besides antiquities the
museum includes various other collections.

Einar Jonsson's Museum houses a full collection of
that sculptor's work. It was built at the expense of the
state, and the sculptor, who is also curator, lives in the
building on a pension granted him by the Althing.

Of Jonsson's work Olive Chapman says:

. . . when . . . I visited the collection . . . I was certainly unprepared for what I saw. The wonder of those
grand conceptions in stone and bronze is beyond my power
to describe. They combine intense strength and power
with real spiritual beauty, and a modern feeling for pattern
and design. The subjects are mostly of a mystical and sym-
bolical nature. He who created them has a message to give
the world, the triumph of spirit over matter.

Lindroth, after pointing out that Iceland may claim
half of Thorwaldsen (Thorvaldsson) since his father
was an Icelander, says: "But Iceland no longer needs to
bargain for a share of him, for she is now possessor of

another outstanding name in the history of sculpture—
Einar Jonsson." Unlike Miss Chapman, he attempts a
critical analysis of Jonsson's work:

This artist can truthfully be said to have created something new on a national basis . . . Just as a longer kenning
or figurative transcription by the skalds sometimes had to
force quite unrelated elements into unity, so Einar Jonsson's
work often symbolizes a general idea through the synthesis
of single details, each one of which signifies a thought or an
idea of its own. And just as the meaning of a kenning, especially to the uninitiated, may not be clear without a re-
capitulating afterthought, so several of the artist's creations
appear a little too palpably to be the products of speculation.
This does not necessarily imply any lack of inspiration,
which, on the contrary, often stands out with great clarity,
and in certain works with soul stirring power.

In Fairmount Park, Philadelphia, there are statues of
the greatest explorers down through the ages. The first
discoverer represented is Thorfinn Karlsefni, by Einar
Jonsson.

CHAPTER V

Medical Services

PUBLIC HEALTH comes under the Ministry of Justice and Ecclesiastical Affairs. It is regulated by a variety of acts and decrees. The Director of Public Health is a qualified M.D.; his position is permanent, does not change with changes of government. Other appointees include a medical officer in charge of tuberculosis who superintends preventive measures, the chief medical officer of the Social Insurance Institution and the director of the State Food Control Institute.

The country has been divided into forty-nine medical districts, each with an officer in charge. In addition, committees and special officers are appointed to carry out regulations or see that they are enforced. For example, there are sanitation committees who supervise disinfection, vaccination, and such animal diseases as are communicable to humans, e.g., tapeworm. They also supervise quarantine regulations on both Icelandic and foreign ships. Local inspectors carry out the work of these committees.

District physicians combine health measures with the regular duties of their profession. However, it is proposed that this dual function be abolished so that the district physicians shall be concerned only with direct public health work.

The medical districts vary a great deal in population and area. About half of them have populations of from one to two thousand. Except for Reykjavik and a few of the larger towns the district physician is frequently the only doctor in the entire area. In extensive and sparsely populated districts the distance from his house to the remotest farms may be as much as seventy miles. Over this he used to make his way, often across mountains or fields of lava, fording the unbridged rivers. Usually such journeys were made on horseback, but in winter the doctor sometimes had to go afoot or on skis. In some places he had to use a motorboat across fjords and bays or around promontories which project out into the open ocean. It sometimes took a doctor days to reach his patient.

Modern improvements are changing this and such journeys are now rare. Today all district physicians are within reach of telegraph and telephone from every part of their respective fields. Bridge and road construction have made rapid progress; automobiles and airplanes are now called into service.

District physicians are paid by the Treasury. The salary is largest in the most sparsely populated districts, ranging from kr. 4500 ($1125) down to kr. 2500 ($625) in the cities. Those who work in remote districts have the twin advantages of more money and lower living costs. Outside of their state work they charge fees, as do all doctors, in accordance with a tariff fixed by the public health authorities. Their total annual income ranges from $1500 to $2000.[1]

Other doctors paid by government funds include professors and lecturers of the medical faculty at the University, permanent appointees in the larger state and district hospitals, and such specialists as the one in charge of the State Free Clinic for Venereal Diseases, the assistant physicians at state hospitals, the school and poor-relief doctors. Those whose services are wholly in the interests of the state receive up to $3000 a year.

There are, of course, private practitioners, including surgeons, gynecologists, neurologists and the like. In the sparsely populated districts, however, most of the doctors are general practitioners. As in some other countries, too, many of the medical students are restricting their work to one specialty and to an urban practice—they find district work unattractive. This trend is causing a fear that there may soon be too many doctors in the cities and not enough to serve the rural population.

[1] These are bank exchange values. On the average throughout Iceland fifty cents will probably buy as much as a dollar will in America. If you do not purchase imported things like southern fruits or London and Paris clothes but live on such home staples as fish, mutton, beef, potatoes and ordinary garden vegetables, twenty-five cents will perhaps buy as much as a dollar buys here. But if you feel that local products are not good enough for you the cost of living in Reykjavik can become even higher than it is in New York.

According to the authorized tariff, district physicians are allowed to charge 50¢ for a simple examination; 75¢ to $1.00 for a thorough one. An extra 25¢ is allowed for visits at the patient's home, and fees may be increased 50% for night calls. The prices are also fixed for surgical operations. They range from 50¢ or $1.00 for slight operations up to $20, with extra fixed charges for attendance on the patient afterwards. The fees are highest for the first few days but are then reduced (75¢, 25¢, 12½¢). In addition to the cost of his taxi, bus or other conveyance, a doctor may charge 50¢ an hour for the first six traveling hours, 25¢ an hour for the next six, and 12½¢ an hour thereafter. This reduction is made for the benefit of those who live in remote districts. For journeys on foot or at night the doctor is allowed an extra 50%. All doctors who receive a salary from the state are bound by these rates.

But the schedule applies only to the native population. Doctors who treat foreigners, however, may not charge higher fees than would be thought reasonable in the patient's native country.

Private practitioners may charge 50% more than district physicians, and specialists 100% more when treating a condition which belongs to their specialty. Private practitioners are dissatisfied with the present tariff scale; no doubt it is sometimes exceeded. This is not very important (from the patient's point of view), for most people in the towns—and only there do we find private practitioners—are covered by mandatory sick insurance, which provides both medical care and hospitalization. Private practitioners are paid an annual fee for each insured person who chooses them; the most popular doctors have up to 1500 insurance clients on their lists. There are pharmacists only in the towns, about fifteen in the whole country. In villages and in the country dispensing is by the government physician who gets his supplies from the State Pharmaceutical Monopoly. Medicines are sold at prices fixed by the Ministry of Public Health and are cheaper than in most other countries. In spite of this the occupation is considered profitable; membership in it—possible only by government license and after evidence of qualification—is coveted.

There are signs of a popular desire for increased state control of the sale of medicines and it is not improbable that the state may take over all imports, even if the present retail distribution is continued.

There are few dentists in Iceland, although this is not because there is nowadays lack of work. The population is too scattered for them to make a living in the rural districts. So they are concentrated in the towns. Many of the rural population feel they cannot afford to visit a dentist until their teeth are entirely decayed; then they buy false teeth. To remedy this condition, many of the younger district physicians are taking up the simpler forms of dentistry.

Generally dental technicians work only in the service of dentists and may not practise independently, but where there are no dentists the technician may make

"No longer can we maintain a splendid isolation." Reykjavik from the air.

artificial teeth under the supervision of the district physician.

Dentists are all private practitioners. There is no fixed tariff except insofar as a tariff has been set for district physicians—dentists may charge 50% more.

For obstetrics the country is divided into 200 districts, with one qualified midwife in each. (Reykjavik, however, has twelve.) Those who are officially appointed receive their salaries from the townships. In rural districts the Treasury pays two thirds and the rural council one third. Their subsidy is fixed at $75 a year in districts of 300 inhabitants or less, with an additional $2.50 for each fifty inhabitants over 300. Annual income from this source may not exceed $375. A 25% cost-of-living bonus applies to salaries of $75 and under.

The patients also pay the midwife at fixed rates. For attending a woman and assisting at the birth of a child, $1.75; for each day she stays with the mother, 62½¢; for visits 25¢. In this way the midwives ordinarily receive $6.25 to $8.75 for each birth. However, the fact that the population is scattered shows plainly in this field. Out of a total of 2500 births a year, some 900 are from Reykjavik—leaving an average of eight births a year for each midwife. Usually they are not dependent on this work but are farmers' wives who are on call when needed. Frequently they are also in charge of vaccination, for each of which they receive 5¢ in the rural districts and about 9¢ in towns and villages.

During the summer eye specialists travel about the

country under the auspices of the Ministry of Public Health, and the people of each village have an opportunity of consulting them at least once a year. Dentists, also, frequently travel about, but they do that as a private venture.

There are only six qualified veterinary surgeons in Iceland, four of them paid by the state and two practising privately in Reykjavik. This is because the scanty population makes it difficult for them to be of service, a great inconvenience when one considers how large a factor animal husbandry is in the national life. Veterinary surgeons receive about the same pay as district physicians but draw additional income from such things as compulsory inspection of all meat exported from the country.

The shortage of qualified veterinarians is to an extent equalized by laymen who have acquired moderate knowledge and skill. Some of these receive small public grants for their work.

All the chief hospitals employ qualified nurses, but private nurses will hardly be found outside Reykjavik. There are school nurses in some of the larger towns and others who are employed in preventive work against tuberculosis. There are some practical nurses whose work is mainly assisting the housewife or running the house if she is ill. They perform a useful service and there might well be more of them.

Masseurs and masseuses have been licensed to practise but the number of independents is decreasing, since many doctors who are specialists in physiotherapy have clinics to which general practitioners recommend their patients. Masseurs and masseuses are paid according to a fixed tariff.

In 1876 the first medical school was founded in Iceland. Up to that time students had to receive their whole medical training abroad, which made for a shortage of qualified doctors. When the University was founded in 1911 the medical school was joined to it and at present is attended by some sixty to seventy students a year. The training requires six years and about ten candidates qualify a year. This has changed anxiety because of shortage to anxiety because of overproduction of medically trained people.

The school of medicine is weak both in facilities for research work and in staff. It cannot stand comparison with foreign medical schools, but it does turn out fairly competent doctors for general practice. A great advantage is that the small classes make for individual attention and students are thereby forced to keep abreast of their subjects. The University hospital is the State Hospital and here students get their practical training. They also attend the various isolation hospitals. Those who wish to specialize continue their training abroad.

Internship for one year is a requirement for all medical students. This can be either in Iceland or abroad. The State Hospital is the one most sought after but it cannot accommodate all the applicants, many of whom therefore go to one of the Scandinavian countries or to Germany. Some have gone to the United States. Most

Icelandic physicians have been abroad for one form or other of graduate study and, as a class, they can stand comparison with those of other countries.

The study of pharmaceutical chemistry has two stages. First, the student must complete three years with a practicing pharmaceutical chemist. Then he must take a two-year course at the Pharmaceutical School in Copenhagen, or at a similar school elsewhere. A few have done this work in Germany.

There are no schools for dental surgeons or technicians and none for veterinary surgeons. Those who want to follow these occupations must study abroad. The dental school at Copenhagen takes one Icelandic student but most of the rest study in Germany.

All of the foregoing professions have their own associations. A list of them will be found in Appendix B.

In 1810 there were only three hospitals in the entire country. There are now 1100 beds in all the hospitals, or about one hospital bed for every 110 persons. About 57% of the beds are in the forty general hospitals.

Some twenty of these general hospitals, however, are only small cottages with two to five beds each, attached to the doctor's residence in isolated districts. There are nine which have more than twenty beds.

The largest of all the general hospitals is the State Hospital in Reykjavik where a hundred-bed capacity has been crowded to accommodate one hundred forty or more patients. It has three main departments—internal medicine, surgery and X-ray. This last department is so well equipped that it attracts the attention of foreign medical visitors. The hospital has two other departments in addition to the main three, one for maternity cases and the other for skin and venereal diseases. In connection with the hospital there is a large and well-equipped laboratory for research in pathology and bacteriology.

On the whole the State Hospital may be said to be equipped according to the demands of modern times, but increased accommodation is urgently needed. The building may indeed be said to be still in the course of construction for although use of it began in 1930 not all of the original plan has been completed.

The second largest hospital is that of the nuns of the St Joseph's order in Reykjavik. This hospital contains 100 beds. Most of the larger towns own fairly good little hospitals with 40 to 50 beds in each; the capital itself has not as yet any hospital of its own, except a small and ancient fever hospital.

Of the special hospitals there are four for tuberculosis, with a total number of 284 beds. The two chief sanatoriums are near Reykjavik and Akureyri. In the neighborhood of Reykjavik there is a lunatic asylum with 180 beds and a leper hospital with 25 beds. The latter was presented to the state by the Danish Order of Odd Fellows in 1898. It is now nearly empty, for the disease is disappearing. The state isolation hospital in Reykjavik has 25 beds, and the above-mentioned fever hospital has 35. With the exception of this last hospital and a tuberculosis sanatorium with 24 beds, which belongs to a charitable society, the state owns and operates all the special hospitals.

Daily fees in state hospitals are from $1.25 to $2.00, which fees are all-inclusive. The state, however, charges from $3.75 to $12.50 for the use of its operating and delivery rooms. Other hospitals charge daily fees of 75¢ to $1.00 (the cottage hospitals) and $1.25 to $2.00 (the larger hospitals) exclusive of medical aid, medicines, X-rays and so on.

Over-all expenses in the State Hospital are about $2.75 a day. In the tuberculosis sanatoriums and the lunatic asylum they amount to just over $1.25. The State Hospital and the two tuberculosis sanatoriums of the state are heated with natural hot water, which is both cheap and convenient.

Since 1919 a health protection institution has been run in Reykjavik by a local nursing society. It is first and foremost concerned with the prevention of tuberculosis, but also has been to a certain extent interested in mother and child welfare. This institution recently had a large growth, and the running expenses are now practically all defrayed with public funds (the Treasury, the municipality of Reykjavik, and the sick insurance of Reykjavik contributing equally). Similar institutions are now being established in all the larger towns; the societies that run them receive grants of public money.

There are a few other institutions concerned with the care or prevention of illness and protection of health. In Reykjavik there is a state deaf-and-dumb school and one asylum for mentally deficient children and women, with accommodation for twenty persons. Another is needed for boys and men, while a third is needed for alcoholics. It is proposed to build both in the near future with the aid of a government subsidy.

The very excellent municipal swimming bath in Reykjavik may perhaps be included with health institutions. The water is supplied from hot springs in the vicinity of the town. Swimming baths with natural hot water may also be found in numerous high and elementary schools throughout the country. It still remains, however, to exploit the numerous possibilities for health resorts provided by the hot springs that are rich in minerals (and some of them radioactive).

There is in Reykjavik an excellent institution for old people, with accommodation for 150, and there are smaller homes in other towns. The only institutions for children are day schools in Reykjavik and elsewhere. It is not infrequent that nursing or charitable societies send children to country homes in summer.

The National Life Saving Association of Iceland, a voluntary organization, operates all over the country. A Society for the Prevention of Tuberculosis established the first sanatorium in 1909 but ceased activities when the state took into its hands the problem of tuberculosis control and cure. The Friends of the Blind Society for Iceland and the Friends of the Deaf work for the assistance and betterment of these handicapped people. There is an active division of the International Red Cross which has taken the lead in general instruction in home nursing, first aid and so on. The boy scout clubs belong to the International Boy Scout movement. The International Order of Good Templars have, for some fifty or sixty years, fought consistently for prohibition of alcoholic beverages. Finally there is the Cremation Association of Iceland which has for its object the substitution of cremation for burial as the general custom of the country.

CHAPTER VI

Health and Social Conditions

VIEWING PUBLIC HEALTH in Iceland today we must remember that only a short time ago conditions were in most respects truly medieval. Like other nations the Icelanders have ghastly stories to tell from the Middle Ages—of the Black Death, of smallpox, of want and starvation. But there are few countries in which a primitive medical situation lasted so near our own day as in Iceland.

In one modern thing of public health significance Iceland was, however, among the pioneers. The Britannica, which does not mention Iceland in this connection, gives the first modern census taken as having been in the French colonies of North America, in what are now the Canadian provinces of Quebec and Nova Scotia, about "the mid-17th century." Then the article gives as the years of first census: Germany, 1742; Sweden, 1748; Denmark, 1769; Spain, 1787; Great Britain, 1801. Iceland's first census was taken in 1703. It showed a population of just over 50,000, which some scholars consider to be only half as many people as the island had contained at its best.

In spite of a very high birth rate (thirty, forty and even fifty per thousand in some years), there were, it is believed, fewer inhabitants at the beginning of the nineteenth century than there had been at the beginning of the eighteenth. Inadequate and poor houses, unsanitary conditions, lack of food, endemic and epidemic diseases thus not only destroyed on a scale corresponding to that of the birth rate but went in excess of it. Similar conditions lasted well into the nineteenth century, except that Asiatic plagues were less prominent and that small-pox was being lessened through vaccination.

During the first three decades of the nineteenth century health conditions improved slowly; there were sometimes whole decades when no progress was made, and there were even years of retrogression. Infant mortality was appalling. Down to the middle of the century one third of all children died in their first year. Mackenzie reports that scarcely any children on the Westman Islands in the period of 1790–1810 lived more than three weeks. Most of them died in one week or less. Measures for mother and child protection have brought this shocking figure down to among the lowest in the world—from forty to fifty child deaths per thousand. Deaths of women from childbirth or diseases related to childbirth are now 3.5 per thousand.

Ordinary epidemics (measles, influenza, whooping cough) often proved fatal to large numbers of people. One epidemic of measles in 1846 killed more than 2000, or thirty-five per thousand; in 1882 measles took some

1700 people, twenty-four per thousand. Epidemics still occur. They are subject to fluctuation because various "foreign fevers," long endemic in other countries, are not endemic in Iceland. Periodically brought into the country they become epidemics. The death rate varies from year to year; but that they are under better control is indicated, for in the last epidemic of measles (1936) only fifty to sixty died from a population of more than 100,000, or less than one person in 2000.

Shortly before 1890 a definite improvement began. Since then the population has steadily increased—the last fifty years 70%, in spite of a continuously decreasing birth rate (about twenty-two per thousand at present) and in spite of an emigration to the United States and Canada amounting to approximately 30% of what the population was in 1890.

Recent economic improvement has been reflected by increased education facilities and a higher standard of living. The effects of prosperity are noticeable even in such things as stature. The last generations have recovered from the stunting effect of poor living and are now, on the average, the tallest of even the tall Scandinavian peoples. Volcanic eruptions, failure of fisheries and of grass crops, or even a combination of these calamities, will not hereafter produce such an effect as formerly upon the health and increase of the people, nor has the world financial depression as yet—it did reach Iceland, though without quite the serious consequences it has had in many other countries.

Iceland has had the doubtful honor of being linked with certain endemic diseases (leprosy, hydatides and tetanus in small children), and in some countries was known to health authorities chiefly because of them. They have disappeared or are disappearing. Tetanus has not been reported of recent years. The Leprosy Acts of 1898 and 1909 provide free supervision and quarantine. Only twenty or thirty lepers are left, most of them old people, and it is probable that the disease will die with them. Typhoid is not banished entirely, but nearly so. Diphtheria is rare; there are few countries with a lower fatality percentage. During the last years it has usually been less than eleven per thousand.

Hydatides was until recently one of the most frequent things that Icelandic surgeons had to deal with. It was reckoned as a low estimate that in 1880 about one in every sixty was afflicted. The Hydatides Acts of 1890 and 1924 include instruction as to the nature of the disease and outline forms of protective measures against it. An important part is the handling of dogs, the curing of tapeworm in dogs. The act is carried out through funds from the sale of dog licenses; by its provisions dogs may be limited in number, or even forbidden entirely, as has been done in Reykjavik. These measures have been so effective that now when medical men from foreign countries arrive to study hydatides, Icelandic doctors have trouble finding an old case or two to show them. Of new cases there are none.

The changeable climate is thought by some Icelandic

medical authorities to be the factor in causing epidemics of colds and other "diseases due to exposure." In this connection is cited a pneumonia rate, considered high by Icelandic medical writers, of about one for each 2000 of population. But this is about the prevailing rate for the entire United States and is only about half as high as the rate for the state of Alabama, which certainly is not climatically one of the most changeable states—let alone one tenth as changeable as Iceland. From the American and other comparisons it would seem, then, that the important pneumonia rate factors may be other than those of climate.

Rheumatic fever is rare in Iceland. Influenza comes about once every two years and is epidemic for about three months.

Tuberculosis has no doubt been in the country since the Middle Ages but was evidently less serious before 1850 than it has been since. That seems strange, for health conditions have been on the upgrade in nearly every other respect. Increased communication facilities within the country and with foreign lands are sometimes blamed for the increase. The disease has been sweeping the country like a protracted and difficult epidemic.

The chief measure used with tuberculosis was to care for patients in special hospitals without cost to them. This, combined with other tactics, seems now to be having some effect. In former years it was not unusual for doctors to treat nearly twenty per thousand of the entire population, and for a time it was one of the chief causes of death. In 1932 the disease reached its peak, with 220 deaths (in a population of, say, 110,000). During 1933 there was a decrease to 173, and in 1934 to 149—which put tuberculosis third in the fatality list, after old age and cancer. This improvement has continued since, except that in 1936 an epidemic of measles and whooping cough seemingly was an aggravation, for total deaths rose to 165. The 1938 tuberculosis rate was less than eight deaths per thousand, but it is still too high.

The health authorities of Iceland are following up every foreign improvement in the care and cure of the tubercular, for they are bent on tempering this affliction. That they are meeting with success is indicated, for the once rather common tuberculosis of the brain is now rare. The present legislation (last amendment, 1929) provides free treatment and maintenance in sanatoriums. Under its provisions children and young people are excluded from contact with the sick. Another revision of the law is contemplated which would put at the disposal of the health authorities funds for research and for additional preventive measures.

Of the venereal diseases gonorrhea is endemic in the towns where numerous cases are brought in by Icelandic and foreign seamen. Almost never is a case found in a rural district. Syphilis is rare; in most cases the infection was acquired abroad. Chancre is unknown. The Venereal Diseases Act (last amended, 1932) lays emphasis on education as to the nature of the ailments, direction for preventive measures against infection and free medical aid. Iceland is a party to an international agreement (Brussels, December 1, 1924) facilitating medical treatment for sailors of the mercantile marine.

Freedom in love affairs and sexual indulgence is undoubtedly no less among Icelanders than among other people, and some nineteen children per thousand are born out of wedlock. The authorities guarantee to mothers of illegitimate children a maintenance allowance from the fathers, and such children have the same rights as those born in wedlock. Strictly speaking, there is no prostitution.

Cancer and other malignant growths account for the deaths up to 150 per year, or one to one and a third per thousand. Persons confined in lunatic asylums number about 3.5 per thousand, which is similar to the other Scandinavian countries. The manic-depressive type is the most common. Suicides are reckoned about one in ten thousand, but this is perhaps a low estimate. At least 300 cases of epilepsy are known, or up to three per thousand. Congenital mental deficiency is comparatively frequent. There are about two per thousand who on this score require permanent support from others.

Following the social upturn around 1890 came an increased realization of the harmful effect of excessive use of alcohol upon health, and a struggle for prohibition started. About the beginning of the present century the annual consumption (in terms of pure alcohol) was officially half a gallon (.55 gal.) per inhabitant, but considerable smuggled liquor did not figure in the statistics.

In 1915 the sale of alcoholic beverages was prohibited, whereupon the medical profession demanded unlimited alcohol for professional use, and this was granted. But not all the doctors proved ethical; some of the druggists were even less so. Then there was foreign economic pressure, particularly from Spain. That country was the largest purchaser of Icelandic salt fish, and prohibition destroyed the market for Spanish wine. Spain protested strongly against this handicap to her foreign trade and against its will the Icelandic parliament in 1921 acceded to her demand, in return for certain tariff concessions on fish. Bootlegging and home-brewing further strengthened the position of the anti-prohibitionists, and in 1935 the law was repealed. There was substituted a State Liquor Monopoly. In 1938 this monopoly sold alcoholic drinks to about a quart (.286 gal.), reckoned in pure alcohol content, per inhabitant.

Narcotic addiction is rare. A secret traffic in drugs does not exist.

Blindness is common, involving about four per thousand of the population, as against 0.5 to 0.7 in other Scandinavian countries. There are about sixty or seventy deaf and dumb. Special schools provide free treatment, maintenance and education.

Dental caries, which in the darkest days of the nation was practically absent, is now one of the commonest troubles. This book tells how in many respects things are better than they used to be; oral decadence is one of the few exceptions and one of the most depressing.

People still live in Iceland who remember when tooth decay was rare, and many remember hearing from parents or grandparents that a little earlier it was wholly absent, except in the trading centers. This could be a mere tale of the good old days; but we have corroboration from two sources, books and archaeology.

There is no literary confirmation from the saga period, but perhaps teeth were so usually good then in northwestern Europe, as well as in Iceland and Greenland, that there was no cause for remark. In the eighteenth century, however, tooth decay was common among the seafaring peoples that traded with Iceland; they noted the tooth health and remarked on it.

Johann Anderson was mayor of Hamburg and used his prominence and influence partly to gather information which he published in his *Nachrichten von Island, Grönland und der Strasse Davis, etc.*, Frankfurt and Leipzig, 1747. He tells in the introduction of that book how he used every care for many years to interview the people best informed about Iceland, fishermen, traders and travelers. Among the things they told him was that the people had remarkably good teeth.

Shortly after the publication of the Anderson compendium Niels Horrebow was sent to Iceland by the Danish government to report on conditions and resources. He found many things so different from Anderson that he wrote, to a considerable extent for purposes of refutation, his own book, *The Natural History of Iceland*, London, 1758 (original Danish edition, Copenhagen, 1752).

While one gets from Horrebow the impression that he was trying to be accurate, one does receive also the feeling that there was a tendency to seek out points for disagreement with Anderson. But on the health of the teeth he agreed; and brings out the point that in the trading centers the condition of the teeth was not so good as among the common people.

As represented from several angles in different chapters of this book, there was negligible commerce with Iceland during, and for some time after, the period covered by Anderson and Horrebow. The small quantities of European food imported were consumed almost exclusively by the traders and by those who served them in the villages.

Today it appears nearly settled, through recent advances of medicine, physiology and dietetics, that it is food which controls the health of the teeth. The people of whom the tradition and the writers speak as possessing the good teeth were in the eighteenth century still living on the diet which had been standard ever since the ninth century—flesh foods (from the sea and from domestic animals) together with milk and its products. There were no gardens, unless in the villages where the people had the bad teeth, so that those with the good teeth were living on a diet in which products of the vegetable kingdom were negligible or absent.

Archaeology certifies the correctness of the tradition and of the books. If truth could be an overstatement, the facts have really overstated the case—they have gone farther than the writers and at least as far as the most extreme tradition. For the archaeologists have shown that tooth decay did not exist (or at least, signs of it have not yet been found) outside the trading villages through several centuries of Icelandic history.

One of the first, and to this day one of the most striking, demonstrations is through a collection of eighty-six Icelandic skulls now at the Peabody Museum of Harvard University. These are from the centuries between the twelfth and fifteenth and are beyond doubt from people the same in blood as those who now live in the country. Not one decayed tooth has been found in the collection.

Seven hundred and even four hundred years ago there was, then, so far as the evidence yet goes, a 100% freedom from dental caries in Iceland, outside the trading centers. It would seem probable that a hundred years ago there was at least a 90% freedom, taking the country through. Today the percentage of those Icelanders who never have a single cavity in any tooth is probably no better than in Paris, London or New York.

The American editors of this book have sought current New York information and opinion with regard to decay of the teeth in the United States. There appears some dispute as to the percentage of those who pass a full life span without developing even one cavity. However, few authorities place victims of tooth decay at less than 90% of the American population. There are specialists, we find, who say that of 1000 who live an approximate three score and ten, 999 will have had more or less tooth decay—that the permanently caries-free are less than 0.1% of the American population.

Toothache, decay of the teeth, is then a fly in the amber to Icelanders when they rejoice in the growth of commerce and of intercourse with the rest of the world during the last seventy-five years.

Heart diseases and apoplexy occur in about the same ratio as in other countries and figure in about two per thousand of the deaths. Diabetes is so rare that it is extraordinary when a doctor finds it.

Accidental deaths are common; the chief occupation, fishing, is dangerous. For that very reason many things are done to protect sailors. Preventive steps include rigorous inspection of ships, establishment of many and good lighthouses, frequent radio bulletins on weather conditions, well-equipped lifesaving stations and so on.

Accident insurance is compulsory. In 1903 it covered sailors on decked vessels; in 1909 and 1917 the scope was widened to all vessels except the very smallest. In 1917 disability insurance was adopted. In 1925 the act was extended to cover almost all laborers on sea and land, with the exception of those in agriculture.

Accident insurance is divided into two classes, one covering sailors, the other industrial workers who are divided into twelve risk-classes, with varying premiums according to the degree of risk. Those outside the limits of compulsory protection may be insured by themselves or by their employers.

Accident insurance is collected when working time of

ten days is lost, the assured receiving a daily allowance which may not exceed three quarters of his normal wage. Payments start one week after the person became unfit for work or stopped receiving wages. The allowance continues until recovery or until a decision has been made as to permanent disablement. The maximum term of payment for any one accident is six months. In addition full payment is made for medical aid and for hospital expenses. Three quarters of the amount spent for medicines outside hospital is also allowed.

Lump payments are made if an accident entails permanent disability assessed at 20% or more. The size of the payment is determined by the degree of disability.

If the accident causes death within a year of its occurrence compensation is paid to a widow or widower, to children, brothers or sisters or to parents. Amounts vary according to the ages of the relatives and the extent to which they were dependent upon the deceased for support.

The costs of accident insurance are borne by the employers.

Analysis of government budgets and of health legislation shows that in 1876 public health expenditures per capita were 7½¢; in 1915, 75¢; in 1934, $3.24; and in the last years up to and above $5.00.

Other legislation has been passed for the improvement of health conditions.

The Medical Practitioners' Act of 1932 provides that no one (even when possessing a diploma) may practise medicine without the permission of the Ministry of Health. License to practise carries with it the obligation of having fees correspond with the official tariff. Advertisements of medicine and of surgical instruments are permitted only when addressed to the profession by letter or when published in medical journals. This makes it hard for a quack to exploit the sick, nor can he easily frighten the well into dread of illness.

The Hospitals Act of 1933 controls the operation of private hospitals which may be run only on certification by the Ministry of Health that they meet acceptable standards.

The General Quarantine and Fever Acts (amended 1933) provide that special precautionary measures must be taken at state expense to protect the country against a variety of "foreign fevers" of an epidemic nature. Entire districts have been isolated successfully, but only in out-of-the-way parts.

Insurance against sickness is compulsory in all towns and thus covers about half the population. It is optional in rural districts. It protects all between the ages of sixteen and sixty-seven, exempting only those suffering from grave, protracted, active diseases. Such people may, however, insure themselves against other diseases and against disablements. Persons older than sixty-seven are also entitled to insurance if they ask for it. Two thirds of the cost is borne by the assured, one third is divided equally between the state and the rural or urban community.

Low rates are charged those who have a taxable income which is less than kr. 4500 ($990). Above this income the rates are double. Benefits cover both members and their children and include full medical aid and free hospitalization. In addition most sick insurances pay three quarters of specialists' fees and support women during confinement.

The Act Concerning Public Support of Sick and Disabled Persons (1936) provides that, insofar as sick insurance and accident insurance does not reach them, free treatments shall be given in hospitals or sanatoriums in cases of grave protracted diseases or disablement. Four fifths of the costs are borne by the state and one fifth by the local community. At present the act is restricted to certain specific ailments; but it is planned to widen the scope to cover any serious illness of long duration.

An Act Concerning Inspection of Food and Other Articles of Consumption (1936) calls for inspection of all such articles whether of native or foreign origin. Investigations are conducted by a public analyst.

An Act Concerning Birth Control and Foeticide was passed in 1935. Under its provisions a woman whose health may be damaged or whose life may be lost in pregnancy must be so informed by the doctor and must be advised as to methods of contraception. It is the duty of doctors to advise women who consult them on contraceptive methods. Foeticides are permitted when certain provisions are carried out (for instance, they must take place in a hospital authorized for that purpose);

they must be justified by certain medical indications and by the social condition of the woman. In other words, medical conditions which alone would be considered insufficient can justify the operation if, in addition, social conditions favor it. Before this act came into force there was a certain amount of confusion, as in other countries, the medical profession being either unable or unwilling to distinguish between operations that were permissible and those which were not. Abortions were forbidden by law but were nevertheless performed. The legalizing of foeticides has resulted in a decrease of such operations. On the average about thirty of these now legal operations are done each year.

The Sterilization Act of 1937 has not so far been put into effect. It provides that the Director of Public Health and a board consisting of three members, one of whom must be a doctor (preferably an alienist), and one a lawyer (preferably a judge), may authorize operations of this kind. Castration is permitted at the request of the person concerned, or of a judge after judiciary decision in cases where unnatural impulses may lead to sex crimes, pyromania and the like, and no other solution can be found. Sterilization may be permitted if a man has some hereditary defect considered transmissible to offspring, if he is a permanent lunatic or has a grave protracted disease and there is reason to believe he cannot support himself or his offspring. Foeticides may be permitted under this act if there is reason to believe that the above-mentioned defects will be reproduced in a child, or if conception is the result of rape. In this last, the woman must have reported it immediately and the case must have been proven before a judge.

Although the foregoing shows that much has been accomplished Iceland is working for still further betterment of her standard of living and an increase in physical well-being. She is already near having the lowest death rate in the world. To achieve international leadership in this field it seems necessary only to bring tuberculosis down to what is normal with other nations and to lower the accident rate which, as said, is high through the risks of a fisherman's life.

It is, of course, clearly recognized that bettered labor and housing conditions play a definite part in the improvement of general health. The housing and labor changes are most of them the products of very recent years.

Organized associations of workmen for the promotion of common interests are of recent date in Iceland; it was not till 1894 that the first society of this kind was formed, the Sailors' Union of the deep-sea fishermen. During the first ten years the sailor union movement progressed slowly and was confined to Reykjavik. In 1897 the Printers' Trade Union was formed, followed, in 1906, by a union of unskilled workers. Since then labor union development has been more rapid.

In 1916 was established the Federation of Labor Unions which at present includes organizations of unskilled workers, sailors, trades workers and socialist bodies (political). There are eighty-three in all, with a total of about 12,300 members.

Until quite recently there have been no permanent employers' organizations except among shipowners, the first being formed in 1894 by owners of decked fishing vessels. But this association was dissolved when the smacks began to be replaced by steam trawlers. In 1916 the Steam Trawler Owner Association was founded. Since then various other employers' associations have been founded and they are now combined in a central organization, the Employers' Association of Iceland, which was established in 1934.

Strikes and lockouts were rare in Iceland before the Great War; when prices began to increase during the war these weapons were used in wage disputes. The central authorities took no part in the quarrels except that a bill was passed by the Althing in 1915 forbidding civil servants to strike. On rare occasions, too, the government has tried mediation in labor disputes. These grew more frequent and violent, so another bill was passed in 1925 providing for a public mediator who serves a term of three years. When labor disputes arise and private negotiations fail, and when the dispute, because of its extent or character, may be considered dangerous to the community, the mediator calls before him representatives of both workers and employers for arbitration.

Labor legislation has moved slowly except, as already

said, in the fishing trade, for industry is still young in Iceland. In various statutes from past times there may be found regulations enforcing Sabbatarianism more or less strictly. Under an act of 1926 all noisy indoor and outdoor work, as well as keeping shops open on sacred days of the established church are, with a few exceptions, forbidden. In 1917 town and municipal councils were authorized to decide the closing hours of shops in their respective municipalities.

Just after the beginning of the present century (1902), payment of wages in cash was made compulsory; an act of 1930 provides that payment of wages shall be weekly. The same act makes it easier for workers to sue employers for wages due.

Inspection of factories and machinery was provided for under an act of the Althing in 1928. It contains various provisions for arrangement of work, protection of life and health, as well as for the inspection of machinery.

During the war wages, though rising sharply, did not keep pace with the increase in prices. Tolerably reliable information regarding wages is available only for unskilled workers and seamen in Reykjavik. These statistics show that not until 1921 did wages reach the same comparative level as the general percentage of increase. Since then there has been less decline proportionately in wages than prices. In settling questions of wages some consideration has been given to the cost-of-living index, but this index does not automatically regulate wages paid.

Using 100% as a prewar index, the cost of living rose to a peak of 346% in 1920 and is now stabilized at around 130%.

Housing costs rose swiftly during the war, for the chief building materials (wood, cement, iron) had to be imported. This led to a housing shortage particularly in Reykjavik where the population grew rapidly through influx from the farms and from other towns. The municipal authorities had a few houses built as an emergency measure but this gave inadequate relief.

Since Reykjavik was most seriously affected a special act was passed in 1917 forbidding the unnecessary raising of rents there. Under this act, too, the giving of notice was restricted and made subject to the legitimate interests of either party, as if the landlord required the property for his own use, or the tenant was at fault through arrears in rent, disturbance of the peace, etc. A rent committee was set up, to which landlords and tenants might apply. The act remained in force until 1926.

In spite of control measures rents went on rising steadily, though not at the same rate as the building costs which, for Reykjavik, are estimated to have increased fivefold between 1914 and 1920, whereas rents had increased threefold or less. Rents continued to go up, however, until they reached a level which made the construction of new dwellings economically possible. This has resulted in building activity. Rents are still high as compared with prewar figures, but the standards of comfort

Formerly houses were built of turf and stone. Present houses are usually of concrete.

have also been raised through the introduction of modern conveniences.

As the housing shortage increased every sort of accommodation began to be utilized, even outhouses and cellars which had never been intended for human occupation. These were more or less unfit to live in, and the same may be said of the jerry-built houses which were run up at the top of the market. For this reason an act was passed by the Althing in 1929 forbidding the use of cellars for dwellings in all towns and villages of 100 inhabitants or more (they never were used much in smaller villages) unless they met a certain prescribed standard. Those which were occupied at the time the act became operative may still be used even if they do not meet standards; but every year the worst of them are to be cleared out and closed until, in the course of twenty years, they have all been done away with.

In 1931 a Workers' Building Plan was enacted whereby the Treasury pays annually into a fund two kronur for each inhabitant of a city and the city pays in an equal amount. The fund is administered by a board of directors who plan the building program and arrange for loans to finance it. The loans are guaranteed by the Treasury and by the municipality, which assures a favorable bank rate.

These houses are all one- and two-family dwellings equipped with modern electrical and other laborsaving devices. Mortgages may be as high as 85% and are redeemable in forty-two years. Amortization and interest total 5%.

However, these houses cannot be acquired by everyone who has the necessary minimum 15% down payment. They are restricted to workers of a certain income group. A childless person who earns more than kr. 4000 ($880) a year cannot buy either type of house. An allowance of kr. 300 ($66) is made for each child up to a maximum annual income of kr. 5500 ($1210). Nor may the participator, whether he has children or not, be owner of property (of any kind) exceeding the value of kr. 5500 ($1210).

Co-operative housing societies have also been formed. They are discussed in the chapter, "The Co-operative Movement in Iceland." In rural districts the old sod houses are rapidly being replaced by concrete or wood.

Other laws which affect health and social conditions are the Education Act of 1916 which provides annual medical examination of all school children, and the Child Welfare Act of 1932 which has established committees in rural and urban communities to safeguard the interests of children.

The attitude of the state toward the poor has changed. A century ago they received little sympathy, much less decent sustenance. Henderson describes for 1814–15 the position of these unfortunates who were billeted by a Danish "poormaster" on farmers, whether they or the farmers liked it. Families were separated; members were placed in different households if not in different districts.

He says that "if husband, or wife, belong to a different part of the island, he is passed on to his native parish, perhaps never more to behold the wife of his youth," and tells of families remaining together in direst need vowing "that famine, and even death itself, would be more supportable than a separation." Other writers point out that poor relief involved loss of civil rights, not only for a man and wife but for their children.

Present legislation is on the assumption, at least tacit, that if you are able and willing to work and cannot get a job it is the fault of the state, of its social organization. By an extension of this principle, or rather of the feeling that is now basic in Iceland, the sick and the old get help not as a charity but as a right. Through laws now in force anyone may claim public relief at his place of residence; families may never be broken up because of poverty; dependence on relief does not entail loss of civil rights.

Out of poor relief as it then was came the beginning of old-age pensions in 1890, for a law enacted then set about the building of a pension fund. By it all farm workers and unskilled laborers between twenty and sixty had to pay small annual subscriptions which were allowed to remain untouched for a period of years. Later, old-age pensions were granted to poor people over sixty, without reducing their civil rights. But the amounts paid were too small to be of real use, so in 1909 a new act was passed which made fund subscription compulsory for every man and woman between the ages of eighteen and sixty. At the same time the fund was granted a state subsidy. The old-age pension was further raised in 1917 and 1933.

At the end of the year 1934 the total number of insured was about 50,000, thus nearly half the population, with 3600 receiving pensions. This arrangement was radically altered by the Social Insurance Act of 1936, according to which a fund was established to secure pensions for those who are sixty-seven or more, and disability pensions for others insured even if they have not reached that age. Disbursements begin in 1948.

By the terms of the Social Insurance Act every Icelandic citizen between sixteen and sixty-seven, resident in the country, is obliged to pay premiums to the fund. This amounts to kr. 7 ($1.75) in towns, kr. 6 ($1.50) in villages with more than 300 inhabitants, and kr. 5 ($1.25) in rural districts. In addition 1% of taxable income according to the Income and Property Tax Act must be paid. The older pension funds are to be paid into the new one as soon as their work is finished.

Exempted from the act's provisions are those who were sixty years old or more when it was passed and those who are provided for by the pension funds for civil servants, for schoolteachers or for midwives.

The amount of pension payments has not yet been decided. Old people who are in need at present are taken care of by the older pension fund which is expected to function until about 1964. In 1937 payments were made to 6402 people.

Unemployment in Iceland has, until recently, been due to the seasonable nature of the chief occupations. Now world conditions are having their effect and lack of a chance to work is a special problem, as it is elsewhere. The state and municipalities have done much to relieve it by various kinds of work and by the establishment of labor exchanges.

Trade-unions which establish unemployment funds are entitled, on complying with certain requirements, to state and municipal support. Some of the conditions are that members who contribute number fifty or more, that they are all engaged in the same or similar work, that the union is domiciled in a town or village and that members are all residents there or in the neighborhood. The bylaws shall contain stipulations as to premiums payable and grants to be made.

Subsidies must never exceed three fifths of the wages paid in the kind of work concerned; they must not be granted to persons concerned in a strike or lockout; nor to such persons as refuse work when it is offered to them, provided that the wages are equal to the rates accepted by the local trade-union.

The Treasury and districts shall each contribute to the unemployment funds of unskilled workers and seamen 50% of the premiums paid by members of the fund, up to kr. 6 ($1.50) for each person insured. To other unemployment funds each shall contribute 25% if the average income in the occupation is less than kr. 3000 ($660), 20% if the income ranges between kr. 3000 ($660) and kr. 4000 ($880), 15% in the brackets kr. 4000 ($880) to kr. 5000 ($1100). No subsidy is to be be paid to higher income groups. Funds are to be under the control of the Insurance Institute and the Ministry of Labor, and bylaws shall be confirmed by the minister of labor.

These are the provisions of the law. No trade-union has yet established an unemployment fund and so for the present the act is inoperative.

CHAPTER VII

The Co-operative Movement in Iceland

As LEGITIMATELY to be inferred from our discussion in Chapter I, Iceland's commercial position during and at the end of the Danish monopoly in 1854 was deplorable. There were no cargo boats, no decent harbors or quays, no roads, no bridges and few public buildings other than churches. Iceland was in effect virgin territory which had to be opened up. A greater handicap even than the poverty was the lack of men with business experience.

But Jon Sigurdsson did not confine himself to the fight for independence. He encouraged young Icelanders to acquire business training and to open local trading companies. He urged the farmers to band together for group buying and selling. Within fifteen years three joint-stock companies had been set up. These eventually failed through inherent defects in their setup, but the experience convinced the Icelanders that co-operation could be a help and a stimulus to trade. They set about developing a better form of association, which finally took the shape of co-operative societies.

The first true co-operative was launched in 1882 when the farmers of Thingeyjarsysla established their county association, *Kaupfélag Thingeyinga.* It is still functioning. Thingeyjarsysla is a rather isolated though progressive district in the north. Here the farmers seem always to have been public-spirited, for they were leaders in the cultural reawakening of the nineteenth century. Their co-operative organization was part of a broad cultural reawakening; it proved, reciprocally, a training school for leaders in other social and political matters.

Kaupfélag Thingeyinga was divided into groups. A farmer might join any group which would accept him. Usually neighbors, relatives and friends joined the same group; and one of them served as manager. He collected all the individual orders and sent them in to headquarters at Husavik, together with a promise to deliver in payment a certain number of sheep or a certain weight of wool. Membership carried with it the responsibility of all that each should keep any promise made; the members jointly assumed the society's liabilities.

When all the orders from the various groups were in at Husavik arrangements were made with a wholesale firm in England to send out the goods required and to take on the products brought in by the farmers. When the ship arrived the farmers brought their sheep or wool to Husavik. Those who delivered more than was needed to pay for their purchases could take the balance in gold or would receive a deposit certificate from the society.

At first this Kaupfélag did not have a store; it merely executed commissions. It was, however, able to pay better prices for farm products and to sell merchandise at lower prices than could the private traders. The success of this venture led to the establishment of similar societies in most parts of Iceland.

The co-operative movement was helped through being linked up with the liberation struggle; for the chief private competitors were Danes. The strife of Kaupfélag Thingeyinga against the Danish trader was bitter. Enterprising and hard, he foresaw that its success meant his own ruin and he put every obstacle in the way. But his policy was looked upon by the Icelanders as one more form of Danish oppression and that stiffened the determination of the society's membership.

This form of co-operation was satisfactory enough in the early days of the movement, but gradually there developed a need for expansion and for change of procedure. The main emphasis was still placed on executing commissions, but some stores were opened. Eventually the commission business was discontinued and stores were opened which sold goods to members and nonmembers alike and where distribution of the profits among the members was made at the end of the year. The chief organizer of this change was Hallgrimur Kristinsson who had studied the co-operative movement in Denmark. He took over a small society, Kaupfélag Eyfirdinga in Akureyri, and built it into the largest in the country—a position it still holds. Thus the first of Iceland's co-operatives and Iceland's largest are both from the north coast, from adjoining counties.

Under the new system the managers ceased to order goods for members; but in other respects the sphere of action and the basic principle remained the same. The managers continued to obtain promises of payment of fixed quantities of articles; each member was bound in responsibility as before.

Reporting on the survey made by President Roosevelt's Inquiry on Co-operative Enterprise, Jacob Baker states for those European countries which he studied:

The very wealthy and the very poor sometimes belong to consumer co-operatives, but the great bulk of their members are workers with reasonably steady jobs and fair pay. The membership of agricultural co-operatives consists almost entirely of small and middle grade farmers . . . The prices in consumers' co-operatives are too high for the very poor because the quality of goods produced and distributed is on a level above their ordinary uses. The very rich do not find in co-operative establishments the luxury goods that they want; and there is in many countries of Europe a feeling of class distinction that makes it unseemly for the well-to-do to be seen going into co-operative establishments.

This paragraph brings out two important differences between the average European co-operatives and those of Iceland. In a country where hardly anyone is very rich and hardly anyone very poor class distinctions based on wealth are necessarily absent. The largest co-operative in

Iceland has among its members day laborers, fishermen, clerks, teachers and supreme court judges, indeed members from all trades and professions. Its dealings are not therefore special to any one income group.

Very important, and seemingly unique in the history of co-operatives, is the fact that in Iceland consumers and producers are united within one society, and the clash of interests which arises in co-operatives of other countries between consumers and producers has thus luckily been avoided. In the Icelandic co-operative societies the producers of one sort of goods are consumers of others, and the consumers of one sort producers of others. The one concession is that when questions concern production only, a separate section of a co-operative is devoted to them.

Even in the early days the all-inclusive form of co-operative society was most popular in Iceland. It combined a consumers' society, a producers' society and a lending society. The working out of this system was the result of the occupational life of the country, the scattered population and the shortage of banks. The society purchased whatever goods were needed in the district, either for consumption or for manufacture. The goods were, if possible, sold for cash, but in many cases they were carried on the books until the products of the farmers and small fishing concerns were ready for the market. This system is continued today and frequently means an extension of credit from six months to a year.

Except for this credit, present-day co-operatives follow approximately the Rochdale plan as devised in England. The principles are:

Open membership and ownership, regardless of race, nationality, politics or religion.

Each member casts one vote, regardless of his investment.

Limited returns on capital, and return of gains to members through yearly dividends.

Regular provision of funds for promotional and educational work.

Cash trading.

Trading at market prices.

Regular provision for building up reserves.

Iceland's consumer refund is as high as any in Europe, for it averages 8%. Baker gives 8% for England, 5% for Sweden, with an effort to standardize at 3%, less than that for Finland, and for the other countries 6% to 7%. Dividends are paid in cash, though about 50% of each member's bonus is put into an endowment fund which is paid out in a lump sum when old age or retirement changes the economic status of the member.

It is now possible in Iceland to obtain every requirement through a co-operative. Goods are sold to member and nonmember alike.

Baker points out that in America co-operative marketing is several times as extensive as co-operative purchasing. The like is true in Iceland, where the main emphasis is on creating new markets although the consumers' interests are well protected. Among other things,

"Eventually the societies opened stores." The Co-operative at Akureyri.

the co-operative movement has resulted in improved quality of goods as well as in their lowered price. In times of financial crises the co-operative has acted as a stabilizer which discouraged speculation in the necessities of life.

To increase the value of farm products most of the societies have built slaughterhouses, and some have added chilling and freezing plants. Some have built modern dairies. They were the first to grade agricultural products and to pay according to quality. In the old days anything was good enough to send to the Danish merchant; now farmers try to produce first-quality goods for the co-operatives.

Co-operatives enjoy certain tax exemptions. For example, a private merchant is taxed at an increased rate with increased income but the co-operative pays the increased rate only on sales to nonmembers.

There are fishing co-operatives. The crew of one or more ships hire or buy a vessel and operate at their own risk. Pay is in proportion to the value of the catch. Their success has been slight—not because the idea is unsound but because operating costs are high.

The co-operative societies had not been long established when the suggestion was made that they should join forces to promote their common interests. The first attempt in 1895 was abortive; a later attempt—the union of Kaupfélag Thingeyinga with two other societies—laid the foundation for the Federation of Co-operative Societies.

Activities of the Federation were originally confined to education and propaganda. Later it took on the grading and sale of meat for export. In 1915 a permanent sales office was opened in Copenhagen. Two years later the head office was moved to Reykjavik and branches were opened in Copenhagen and New York, though the latter was moved to Leith after the war. The scope of activities has constantly increased. Agricultural and marine produce were added to the sale of meat. A purchasing department was opened for the benefit of the societies and in 1917 a wholesale house was established in Reykjavik. An office was maintained in Hamburg for central European trade until 1932.

Branching out still further, the Federation began to operate some factories, for the dual purpose of giving new outlets to producers and securing lower prices for consumers.

The Federation now comprises a membership of forty-six co-operatives with more than 14,000 members—i.e., every ninth inhabitant is a member of some co-operative belonging to the Federation, and membership is increasing rapidly. In 1937 its turnover was $6,400,000. It controls the entire export of frozen mutton, about 90% of the total meat export, about 80% of the wool export and about 85% of the total export of agricultural products. It handles about 20% of the imports.

New conditions develop new methods. The Federation has been alert in this field, as will be obvious from one example, the handling of mutton. Before the end of the last century sheep were sold on the hoof to England. When later British legislation forbade the importation of live sheep the Icelanders slaughtered the animals at home and sold the meat salted, chiefly to Norway. Careful handling and grading gave it a high reputation; but after 1920 the increase of meat production in Norway diminished the Icelandic market. The Federation then established freezing plants in all the chief meat-producing districts. Mutton is now shipped frozen to England. It is gaining a reputation as a quality article in the world market.

Since 1920 the Federation has had an auditing department which surveys the financial position and trading of the societies. This department has been able to co-ordinate activities and to improve accounting methods.

Because the Federation was originally formed as an educational and propaganda institution, it arranged during its first years lectures throughout the country designed to bring the merits of the system to the attention of as many people as possible. It also publishes a journal, *Samvinnan* (Co-operation), which began in 1907 as a quarterly but is now issued monthly. In 1917 it founded a school which prepares students for work with the societies. The course is two years, and about twenty-five graduate each year. This is more than can be absorbed by the societies, and many have taken places outside of the movement where they have proved of great value to it.

Co-operation in housing is a logical extension. The

societies do not receive the subsidy which we have discussed in the chapter on health and social conditions, but they benefit by the fact that the government guarantees their loans. Through this guarantee money may be borrowed at rates of interest more favorable than can be secured by private builders.

Throughout the country as a whole the societies build detached and semidetached houses for their membership. In Reykjavik, however, the Working Men's Building Society prefers apartment construction. The blocks are walk-ups of two stories and basement. They are built with a garden and supervised playground in the center; apartments are usually four or five rooms with a kitchenette; they are equipped with the most up-to-date electrical and other laborsaving devices; and there are certain privileges, such as the use of a laundry in the basement. The first was built in 1932 and others have been erected since then. There are long waiting lists of applicants for membership so that if a member wants to sell his apartment he finds a purchaser instantly.

As with similar co-operatives in the other Scandinavian countries, monthly payments include interest, amortization, maintenance and insurance. When the apartment is paid for monthly payments are decreased and cover maintenance and insurance only. Baker says of Sweden that the effect of co-operative enterprise is apparent in all housing, since private builders who charge higher rents must justify them by more modern improvements. In Iceland the co-operative buildings embody every modern improvement that a private builder could suggest. The effect, therefore, has been a lowering and a stabilization of rents.

One of the differences between the co-operatives of Denmark and Iceland is brought out through a statement by Baker:

In Denmark the farmers make long-term joint borrowings to establish their organizations, and when these obligations are paid off, twelve or twenty years later, they liquidate the whole enterprise and take out the money they had invested in member shares. They do not approve of handing on to the next generation or age-group a debt-free structure for which the previous generation has paid. The younger co-operators then start anew, arranging their own loans, to be paid off by their own efforts.

In Iceland this short-term organization does not enter the picture. Co-operatives are built on long-term plans. When a member dies his share automatically goes to his widow, who may continue membership or not as she sees fit. If a man leaves no widow his share is liquidated and divided among his heirs; but there is nothing to prevent those heirs from reinvesting the money with the co-operative. In this the Icelanders are more nearly in agreement with the Swiss, who look upon debt-free structures as social capital.

CHAPTER VIII

Agriculture

THE GEOGRAPHICAL POSITION of Iceland limits the vegetation which can thrive there and thus prescribes the type of agriculture which may be pursued.

Several places in this book attempt significance through comparison with other lands and perhaps we might try it here. We compare, then, in temperature those cities in Iceland and in North America which have the largest gatherings of Icelanders, Reykjavik with nearly 40,000 people and Winnipeg with perhaps 6000.

The Winnipeg average for the year is just at freezing, 32° F. The Reykjavik average is seven degrees above freezing, 39° F. The coldest for Winnipeg since Icelanders began to live there was −47.6° F. The coldest for Reykjavik in the same period was −6.7° F. The hottest in Winnipeg was 108.2° F.; the hottest in Reykjavik 78.3° F.

Comparing Reykjavik with New York instead of Winnipeg, we have it that the lowest New York City temperature, −14° F., is seven degrees colder than the lowest of Reykjavik, and the lowest New York State temperature, $-52°$ F., is forty-five degrees colder than Reykjavik. The coldest we find recorded for a town in Iceland is $-33°$ F. The coldest for a town in the United States is $-68°$ F. The average temperature of Reykjavik for January is about the same as that of Milan or Philadelphia.

Speaking generally, Iceland has a moist, insular climate with comparatively mild winters and cool summers. The average annual temperature in Reykjavik in the southwest is, as said, $39°$ F., and that of Mödruvellir in the north is $36.5°$ F. The mean temperature of the warmer summer months exceeds $52°$ F. in few or no places. (July in San Francisco averages $58°$.)

The Icelandic climate is particularly variable. During midwinter the temperature may be several degrees above the freezing point with fine weather, while in summer there may be cold spells with snowfall. Precipitation varies greatly with season and locality. In the southeast the annual rate is about twenty inches; in some northern districts it is only four inches. These uncertain conditions, especially in spring and summer, make agriculture difficult.

Nevertheless, since the early days of colonization, husbandry has been the chief occupation of the people. Formerly it constituted almost their only means of livelihood. Now the development of the fisheries and other occupations is decreasing the numbers on the land, though better methods have increased the amount of farm produce.

Iceland has an area of 40,437 square miles, three fifths of which are uninhabited—the highlands in the interior and the mountain ranges branching out from them, which are for the most part useless, being glaciers, drift-sands, mountain wastes or lava fields with little or no vegetation. But though unfertile on the whole these highlands are not all equally barren and some are used as mountain pasture for sheep and horses, which in spring are driven inland and left to their own devices during the summer months. In many parts of Iceland horses feed out all the year and sheep much of the year.

The total area of inhabited land amounts to about 9,389,800 acres. Of this only 108,840 acres are cultivated (i.e., manured homefields, vegetable gardens and irrigated meadows). Of the rest some 494,200 acres are forest land, mostly brushwood, which has until quite recently been used as winter pasture for sheep; and some 8,648,500 acres are grazing grounds, a considerable part of which is unfit for cultivation.

Icelandic farms stand apart and are isolated, each within the borders of its own land. They are seldom found in proper villages, but not infrequently two or three or (rarely) even more farmhouses are built together and the estate parcelled out between them.

Many of the farms are large, probably averaging near 1500 acres, but most of this is uncultivated land, some with scanty or no vegetation. The average cultivated area per farm is about fifteen acres, and that of meadowland about seventy-five acres. As the uncultivated tracts are so extensive in comparison with the cultivated, the value of a farm does not depend on its size but on the quality of the soil. While it is known that the total area of manured homefields is near 80,000 acres and that of vegetable gardens near 1200 acres, meadowlands, forests and rough grazings have not yet been exactly surveyed.

The general survey of land values is made every ten years. The last survey (1930) showed land and buildings valued at $11,694,250. The average price of a farm is a little over $1750.

Four fifths of all the farms are privately owned, the rest being state property. Private farms represent about five sixths of the total value of farm lands. This division has not always existed. In 1695, for instance, of 4058 farms only forty-seven belonged to Icelanders, the rest being owned by king and clergy. At the middle of the eighteenth century about one half of the country was either national estates, church lands or farms owned by the bishops' sees. But towards the end of the eighteenth century and during the first decades of the nineteenth all farms belonging to the sees and a great many national estates were sold to private owners. In 1905, subject to various conditions, the government was authorized to sell all national estates and in 1907 all church lands.

About one half (48%) of the farmers are freeholders; the rest are tenant farmers. Of the latter about three fifths are tenants of private persons, the remainder renting publicly owned lands. Of late years the number of freeholders has increased, that of the tenant farmers decreasing in the same proportion.

Formerly no agricultural implements were used except primitive hand tools; all overland travel and transportation was by horse. Now, however, more and more farmers are acquiring ploughs, harrows and other implements to work the soil. Several farmers join together to buy tractors and take turns in using them. An ever-increasing number are buying mowing machines, horse rakes and hay tedders. Trucks are replacing pack horses. This revolution is now at its height, and farmers hope to complete during the next few years the shift from old and primitive forms to the most advanced methods used in other countries.

Down to the end of the nineteenth century there was no appreciable cultivation of the soil; with the beginning of the present century enterprising farmers went into larger-scale production. The Treasury subsidized this to a small extent and indeed had done so since 1885. No great progress was made, however, until the Althing passed the Cultivation of the Soil Act in 1923. Under this subsidies were given for the principal kinds of improvements in soil cultivation, and since then annual votes have been about $125,000, or a total of between $1,500,000 and $1,750,000 for such grants. The major achievements are outlined in Appendix C, Table 1.

It will be seen from this table that extensive cultivation did not begin until 1925, or immediately upon the coming into force of the Cultivation of the Soil Act. Since then more has been accomplished in one year than previously in a decade. Most of the farmers have made at least a start. Table 2 in Appendix C shows the area of cultivated land and crops for the same period. The table also shows that the size of homefields and the crops of hay have been almost doubled from the beginning of the century. Haymaking in wild meadows has decreased, as might be expected, since many farmers who have enlarged their homefields have stopped using the poorest meadows. The potato crop has increased fourfold and should increase more, for Iceland still must import about one third of her needs.

In 1936 an act was passed providing for the establishment of new farms on unoccupied land and for the formation of farming colonies on co-operative principles. Under this act the government is authorized to enable the greatest possible number to obtain farms in the country where animal husbandry and agriculture can be chief occupations. Public grants are made to those who establish new farms and co-operative colonies. The grants are not repayable but are looked upon as subsidies, the full value in due course being handed down to the farmer's successors. From the Building and Colonization Fund first-mortgage loans may be given up to 7/17 of the original cost. In addition the Treasury may grant an equal amount towards defraying building and cultivation expenses.

To understand the rapid changes which are taking place in rural districts we might first discuss the old-fashioned farm. To every one of them belong a homefield (*tun*), meadows, home pastures and mountain pastures. The homefield is cultivated land, most frequently situated around the dwelling house and the livestock sheds. In former times it was more or less hummocky and was cultivated only to the extent that manure was spread on it once every year. As a rule homefields were un-hedged and badly cultivated, and crops were poor. Now they are cultivated with modern machinery and are fenced. Most farms have vegetable gardens.

Formerly all houses were built of turf and stone. The dwelling itself (*baer*) most frequently consisted of a number of turf buildings joined together. The sleeping room (*badstofa*) was usually paneled with wood, whereas the other buildings were not. The cowshed was frequently attached to the dwelling; the sheep pens and stables were small huts scattered about the homefield.

All the books we have consulted praise the hospitality of the people who dwelt in these "rude" houses, but Henderson was nearly or quite the only one who sug-gested they be contented with their lot. Traveling in 1814–15 on behalf of a Bible society, he was frequently asked by Icelandic farmers about conditions in rural England. As he tells in his book, he did not want to draw invidious comparisons and found a neat way out of his dilemma, pointing out that man's stay here on earth was brief and that the soul's welfare, rather than the body's, was the prime consideration.

The modern Icelander does not believe that there is a necessary conflict between the welfare of the body and the soul. There are now few of the old farmhouses left.

The period 1910–30 saw their number diminished by one third. In the 1930–40 decade they were disappearing almost completely. Present structures are usually concrete and are equipped with modern conveniences, including electricity and central heating. Often the heating is mainly through natural hot springs, electric heat being used as an auxiliary.

All farming is based on the cultivation of grass. The hay from the homefield is used for dairy cows and then for other cattle, while horses and sheep (insofar as they do not graze out in winter) are fed on a different type of hay which grows in the wild meadows. During the last fifteen years the yield of homefield hay has been doubled; that of meadow hay has remained stationary.

As we said before, the potato crop does not satisfy the home market. In 1936 the Althing passed an act to encourage production by granting subsidies (for 1936–38) to those growers who showed a larger output those years than for 1935; by fixing the minimum price of potatoes; by establishing a state wholesale business in this commodity and by reserving for the state the sole right of importing foreign potatoes.

Here and there throughout the country are extensive bogs yielding a fair quality peat that is used for fuel, especially in the rural districts. During the present century, up to the Great War, more than 20,000 tons were dug each year. During the war the quantity dug reached a maximum of 48,000 tons, due to the high price of coal and the risk about getting it to the country. Peat output declined to 14,000 in 1935 and has continued dropping since.

That the use of peat declined instead of growing with the increase in population has several reasons. People have more money now than before the war and are better able to purchase coal from abroad. Roads have improved and have been extended so that trucks are used instead of pack horses for bringing coal from the harbor to a farm. Hot water piped to buildings has decreased the need for fuel. Cities have developed municipal electric plants with current so cheap that it is used for cooking as well as for light, and even for heating, particularly on chilly days that come in a generally warm part of the year. Many farmers have developed their own small electric plants, usually through water power. Between large developments and small individual (farmer) production, Iceland now has probably a higher percentage of electric cooking than any other country in the world.

The forests (brushland most of them would be called in America) are used not only for sheep runs but also for fuel. During the first decade of the present century it is considered that 700 tons of firewood were cut, on an average, every year. In 1918 this reached a maximum of 2600 tons but has decreased until it has now been at about 1300 tons for the past few years.

The first hothouse was built in 1923. Now such buildings cover an area of 55,000 to 65,000 square feet. They are chiefly used for growing flowers, tomatoes and cucumbers. They are kept at optimal temperatures by piped hot water from the thermal springs. In some places the hot water is conducted through the soil to warm it for plants which are in other respects grown in the usual way out of doors.

However, no more than a beginning has been made in the use of subterranean heat for agriculture. There are great possibilities.

The livestock consists mainly of sheep, cattle and horses, mostly descended from animals brought by the settlers a thousand years ago from Norway, Ireland and Scotland.

In proportion to the number of inhabitants, Iceland has more sheep than any country north of the equator, six to each person, whereas in Bulgaria (which comes next) the average is only 1.5 per capita. (Iceland is, of course, surpassed in this respect by Australia and New Zealand.)

The Iceland sheep is of Norwegian origin and is of the sort most common in northern Europe (*Ovis brachyura borealis pall*). It is comparatively small, with long, flowing wool that reminds you of Angora, and is a hardy and frugal-feeding breed.

Icelandic cattle vary greatly in size, color and yield. From the colonization down to about thirty years ago little was done to improve the stock through rational breeding. It is better for milk than for meat. The average annual milk production per cow is estimated at 5292 pounds (2400 kg.), though a few may yield over 8820 pounds (4000 kg.). So far as has been examined to date, the butterfat content runs between 3½ and 4%.

Compared with the number of inhabitants, horses are more numerous in Iceland than in any European country, more than one to every three persons. In the Baltic countries (Lithuania, Latvia and Esthonia) which come next, they run no more than one for every three or four persons. A chief reason why horses are so numerous in Iceland is that, until lately, they have been almost the only means of overland communication. In some districts they are also reared for export.

The Icelandic horse is small, averaging from four to five feet in height. They are rather shaggy; do not require much food; are wonderfully sure-footed, persevering, keen-sighted and gentle.

Details on cattle, sheep and horses, will be found in Appendix C, Table 3.

At present there are in Iceland about 100 cattle breeding and inspection societies with a membership of about 2300 farmers who own about 11,000 cows. The average milk yield has been increased by 882 pounds (400 kilos) since the foundation of the first societies thirty odd years ago. This must be considered good when it is remembered that the cows are fed chiefly on hay. The societies select animals for breeding purposes, keep records of fodder and milk and measure butter content of the milk. At present over one third of all cows are owned by the cattle-breeding societies.

There are eight sheep-breeding farms in the country. They keep select stocks which they try to improve through breeding and then sell to farmers. There are

*The Iceland sheep has long wool and is a hardy
and frugal-feeding breed.*

about fifty horse-breeding societies for improving both the treatment and the breed of horses.

All these societies receive annual grants from the Treasury, totaling about $15,000. These are made in accordance with the provisions of the Livestock Breeding Act of 1931. Under the same act the government makes grants to livestock exhibitions which are held as follows: sheep shows in each district every fourth year, horse shows every third year, cattle shows (held by each cattle-breeding society) every fifth year.

There are some goats, pigs and poultry; but they are comparatively few and no special measures have been taken for their advantage.

An explanation of why there are so few chickens is one of the things you are likely to hear from fellow travelers before reaching Iceland, if you come by steamer from Scotland and have on board, as usually would be the case, several who have made the voyage before. Part of the explanation will be that Icelanders do not like chicken—that it is considered by them inferior to the other domestic meats and to fish. Then it is said that Icelanders feel about chicken eating somewhat as American doughboys must have felt about frog-leg eating when, during the war, they spoke of the French commonly enough as "Frogs."

These explanations are on the right track. Formerly, to most Icelanders (and even now to many of those who do not live in the cities) chicken eating was on the border of things that just are not done. Now, however, in the hotels of the bigger cities chicken is a common dish, as well as in the homes of many city families.

Breeding of furred animals (especially the white fox and the silver fox) has increased a great deal of late years. A special government adviser has been appointed.

We have said that fewer people are now engaged in agriculture than before. The whole increase of the population, and about 6000 persons in addition, have gone over to other occupations since the close of the last century; but in spite of this the total production has increased. Table 4, Appendix C, makes this very clear. For example, it may be seen that mutton production per agricultural worker has increased by about 69%; garden production by about 180%.

The chief agricultural exports are mutton and lamb, wool and hides. Some cheese has also been exported of late years. All other milk and milk products are consumed within the country. The value of exported agricultural goods has been steadily on the rise—from $1,175,000 in 1930 to $2,552,500 in 1937. This increase is due both to higher prices and increased quantity of goods. The greater part of the agricultural production is, however, consumed in the country.

Many farms are so situated as to enable the farmers to supplement their incomes from other sources. Some of these are:

Fishing in lakes and rivers. During the last five years the average annual catch of salmon (of legally prescribed size) has been about 17,000 and of trout 440,000. There are comprehensive regulations, as for closed seasons, modes of fishing, artificial breeding. Salmon fishing brings many sportsmen to the country in summer.

Sealing (hair seal) is carried on to some extent in various places around the coast, the yearly catch amounting to some 340 adults and 3800 young.

The eider duck is protected all the year round for the sake of its down. Farms where this down is gathered in any quantity are considered among the best landed properties. The average national yield is about 8000 pounds.

Most of the down is exported as prime Iceland eiderdown; if there is any grading it is according to the place from which it comes and the extent to which it has been cleaned. In the main, however, it is exported uncleaned. Germany is the largest purchaser; but considerable amounts are taken by Denmark, Norway, Sweden and Switzerland. During the last ten years hardly any has come to the United States. In all countries the chief use is for pillows, quilts and sleeping bags.

On the headlands seafowl abound. The usual way to catch them is: A man goes down a precipice by means of a rope. He has a net attached to a long pole. When the birds rise from the ledges they are caught in the net and are killed at once. During the past few years the annual catch has averaged around 150,000 birds.

The chief farmer society is the Agricultural Association of Iceland which celebrated its 100th anniversary in 1937. It employs advisers in cultivation, market gardening, horse breeding, cattle breeding, sheep rearing, hatching and breeding of fish spawn. It runs an experimental station at Samsstadir in Fljotshlid and a vegetable station at Laugarvatn. It has also experimented with fodder for milch cows and sheep.

In addition, the Association sees to the carrying out of various laws and inspects most agricultural work subsidized by the Treasury. It is, therefore, really a government department now, though it was built up from the farmers' agricultural societies. There are 216 parish agricultural societies which form joint unions comprising one or more judicial districts. There are ten such unions at present. They take the lead in various district improvements. They elect representatives for the Agricultural Conference in which is vested supreme power for all matters concerning the Agricultural Association. The conference is made up of twenty-five representatives and meets every other year.

The Association receives an annual subsidy of $40,000 from the Treasury, but the conference makes the estimates for expenditures. The conference also elects the governing board of three, which board appoints a managing director.

In the chapter on education we referred to agricultural schools. There are two, one at Hvanneyri in Borgarfjördur (southwest Iceland) and the other at Holar in the north. Each of these accepts from forty to fifty students for two-year courses. They are both state schools. Model farms are run in connection with them.

Recently the University of Iceland established an industrial research laboratory, one department of which is to work directly for the benefit of agriculture. This institution has just been opened and can hardly be said to have begun its work. But high hopes are entertained for its usefulness.

The Farmers' Bank of Iceland, operated by the state, was established by an act of Althing on June 14, 1929. Its chief business is to make loans for various enterprises connected with agriculture. It has six departments:

1. Savings and trade-loan, which accepts deposits and transacts ordinary bank business.

2. Hypothecation, which grants loans against mortgages.

3. Cultivation fund, which grants loans for cultivation and improvement purposes.

4. Building and improvement fund, which grants loans at a very low rate of interest for rebuilding farmhouses.

5. New settlement fund, which grants favorable loans for the establishment of new farms.

6. Furred animals department, which grants loans against mortgage for the breeding of fur-bearing animals.

Until the establishment of this institution, the farmers in Iceland had no access to capital and were thereby handicapped in developing progressive agricultural and housing measures.

The amount expended by the Treasury on agricultural matters has increased enormously during the past sixty years—from $600 in 1876 to $459,250 in 1935.

CHAPTER IX

Fisheries

IN MOST island countries fisheries play an important role. For Iceland the role is decisive.

The scientists tell that once upon a time there was a land bridge connecting the American and European mainlands by way of Greenland and Iceland. This is now represented by a submerged ridge from which project Iceland and the Faroes, Iceland rising nearly 6000 feet above sea level.

There is another connection between the New and Old worlds, the Gulf Stream. From one branch of this stream, the Irminger Current, it results that the country is nearly surrounded by warmish waters, 33° to 57° F., as well as that the climate is milder than would be expected from geographical position.

There is another current, polar in character, which comes from the north and strikes the north and east coasts where the temperature of the sea at its surface may drop nearly to 28° F.

Because of these two currents Iceland has two different types of marine plant and animal life, the boreal associated with the Gulf Stream and the Arctic related to the polar current. The principal food fishes are affected by these conditions. The cod, saithe, haddock, herring, halibut and others spawn in the warm-water area off the south and southwest coasts in the months from February to May. The pelagic eggs and larvae, when hatched, drift with the warm water up to the colder parts of the coast, richer in food, where they find excellent growing conditions. At maturity they return in large shoals to the spawning grounds in the south. The fisheries industry is based on these conditions.

During the spring, summer and autumn the fisheries deal mainly with recovering fish which come from the spawning grounds in search of food. Later in this chapter the herring fishery will be described as an example.

The Icelandic fishery is as old as the nation itself. The vikings who came as settlers brought with them the technique of their native countries. Though the industry was always recognized as of value, it did not become really important until Roman Catholicism was adopted and fish gradually replaced meat on the tables on set days of the week and during set times of the year. To around 1300, fishing was only a spare-time occupation. Shortly thereafter an export trade was begun with the sale of wind-dried fish to the Hanseatic traders of Bergen. Bases of operation were established at places on the coast called "ver" in the neighborhood of the great fishing banks. Experience soon taught that the industry is seasonal and that there are times when it is very profitable. These determinations were steps in the establishment of the present industry.

Around 1400 there was still further progress. Up until then the hand line was the only fishing tackle. When the English about this time began to use the long line the Icelanders adopted the invention and it has been important down to today. Shortly after the English came the Germans who had a slightly different technique; Iceland fishermen adopted from them what seemed advisable.

The fisheries pioneers, so far, were the clergy. The Church was already rich; in the fisheries the clergy found a chance to gain additional wealth. This movement progressed steadily until the Reformation (about 1550), when the riches of the Church were confiscated by the Danish crown and the fisheries abandoned. Thus the Danish monopoly cast its shadow upon the fisheries, as it did upon every other phase of national life, until the era of free trade began again in 1854.

The history of Icelandic fisheries falls into three main periods.

The first, or coastal, period lasted from 874 until about 1800—the use of open boats with hand line and long line. The fishermen rarely ventured out into the open sea; they cultivated the fjords and the nearest of the offshore banks.

In the nineteenth century the second period began, when rowboats were replaced with decked sailing vessels. There was no improvement in technique—the tackle was still primitive but the vessels could reach more distant grounds and could stay out for several days, pursuing the fish shoals.

The last period began just before the end of the nineteenth century when the first experiments were made with steam trawlers and, just after 1900, with motorboats. Since then, and down to the present, the trend has been towards greater expansion both with regard to number of boats and excellence of equipment.

The development of new grounds has ushered in a new era. In 1936, for instance, Icelandic vessels were:

Steam trawlers	38	tonnage	13,091
Other steamships	30	"	3,638
Motor vessels	286	"	7,006

The above-listed motor vessels are those of twelve gross tons and over. There are in addition some 600 to 700 smaller motorboats, but no longer any sailing vessels.

Of some 120,000 population, about 7000 people are employed in the fishing fleet. With their families this makes about 25,000 who are directly supported by the fisheries.

In spite of the small number employed Iceland is one of the greatest fishing countries of the world. An analysis, as compiled from figures of the International Fisheries Statistics, will be found in Appendix D. It shows that the catch by Icelanders is per capita more than seven times as great as that of Norway, which ranks first on total quantity.

On their home grounds the Icelanders have eleven rivals, of whom the Germans and the English are the most important. Nevertheless the Icelanders take about half of all the fish caught off their shores. In different years Icelandic waters produce from 17% to 21% of the total fishing output of Europe. In comparison with European populations the Icelanders are only one fifth of one per cent; yet they catch about eight per cent as much fish as all the fishing peoples of Europe. Wording it differently, their per capita fishing take is approximately forty times greater than the European average.

Icelandic steam trawlers, which range between 300 and 400 gross tons, are modern power vessels equipped with tackle called otter trawl. This is most effective; several tons of fish may be caught in an hour or less. Most of the trawlers are equipped with radio, echo sounder, direction finder and other navigational instruments.

Trawlers work on a routine. The one we are about to describe is coming into Reykjavik in September. It is full of frozen fish, for the hold is refrigerated to preserve freshness for the European cities. When the ship berths the crew go ashore, but only for an hour or two; then work begins again. Out of the bay she steams, for she is going to make a few final hauls during the night in order, if possible, to secure more of the commercially valuable plaice. At dawn a course is set for the open sea. Four or five days later she is in the docks of Hull or Grimsby or —when the catch is specially suited to the German market

—in Wesermunde or Cuxhaven. When the fish have been landed the trawler proceeds into the North Sea and northward into the open Atlantic. After some days the highest peaks of the Icelandic mountains reach out of the sea, the echo-sounding device begins to register bottom and the trawler is again on the banks.

Once more the equipment is made ready for use and the rest which the crew have been enjoying is over. Work is carried on at high pressure, with the captain laboring hardest of all, for the running cost of the vessel is $300 a day. The men function with speed and efficiency. The trawl is hauled up every hour and machines take the catch on deck. Then it goes right back into the sea, for every second counts. If the equipment is not in good condition skilled workmen repair or replace.

During the hauls the crew sort the catch according to species and size. Every effort is made to get catches for which a market is waiting and to prepare fish to meet the demands of the markets in which they will be sold. There is continuous radio contact both ashore and with other trawlers; market reports are broadcast. For, important as it is to fish hard, it is just as important to land the catches at the right market on the right day.

Techniques differ according to season. In April, for instance, the chief interest is in the cod on the rich banks in the warm area and in the preparation of klipfish. When the cod are on deck heads, intestines and the greater part of the spinal column are removed. The fish is carefully washed and salted and is later taken ashore for further washing, drying, sorting and packing for the world markets.

Long-line fishery has still another technique. Whether steamships or motorboats are used, the main work consists of baiting the hooks and many thousands of them are put into the water at one time. Over 200,000 large cod have been caught in a single day by long line off the Westman Islands. In exceptional cases there may be a fish on every other hook of a line that is one and a quarter miles long.

Next in importance to the cod is the herring. This fishery depends on shoals migrating for food. Therefore it takes place chiefly in the very cold waters off the north coast and chiefly during July and August, though there is some activity in June and September. One of the greatest world centers for this fishery is the little town of Siglufjördur. During the herring season its normal population of 2500 swells to nearly 10,000 and there are sometimes as many as 200 ships in its harbor at one time. People come from all parts of the country to engage in this occupation or in others connected with it. It is almost impossible to rent a small room; wherever meals are being sold every seat is taken.

At Siglufjördur five large herring meal and oil factories hum with activity, and there are numerous other factories along the coast. Ship after ship brings in its catch. Curing methods differ according to the preferences of the countries to which it will be exported, and

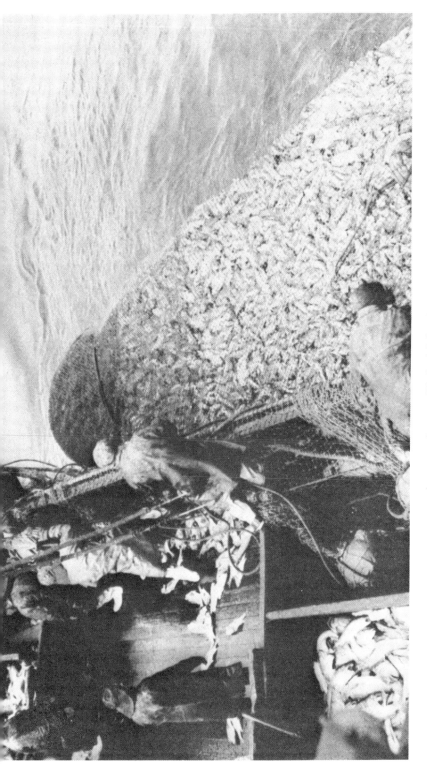

A purse-seine net filled with herring.

there are many countries—the United States, Sweden, Denmark, Germany, Poland, the U.S.S.R.

Such herring as are not up to standard are put into large tanks attached to the oil and meal factories. It is only a minute or two from the time the herring leaves the tank until it has been converted into meal and oil.

Herring oil is used in the manufacture of soap, margarine and explosives. The meal is fed to cattle at home and abroad—Germany is a considerable purchaser.

Outside the fjord, and therefore north of the Arctic Circle, there is tense activity when the weather is good. Trawlers and long-line vessels pay no attention to the cod, for only the herring matters. Each ship carries two specially designed boats. The purse-seine tackle is kept in these boats. While the midnight sun glows red on the northern horizon the crew keep a lookout for telltale signs of herring shoal in the distance.

When a shoal is discovered, with thousands of black backs crowding the surface of the water, the vessel quickly makes for it and the crew mans the special boats. The herring are now feeding upon small crustaceans. The shoal is surrounded with a purse seine and the bottom closed up by a pull from the boat. The mother ship arrives; machines take the fish from the seine and store it in the hold. Sometimes the catch is so large that the vessel cannot take all of it. If there is no other vessel around that needs the surplus it is put back into the sea. The course is then set for port and the crew may sleep a few hours—they intend to go out again soon and fish while they can; for there will be stormy days when the Icelandic boats, and also the Swedish, Finnish, Lithuanian and other vessels must seek shelter from wave and wind. Then little Siglufjördur becomes a cosmopolitan city with foreign crews and a babble of tongues.

A few years ago Icelandic fishermen were behind their rivals in the plaice fishery. They were getting about 75% of the herring taken off Iceland, about 50% of the cod, but only about 7% of the plaice. Now, however, motorboats equipped with the so-called Danish seine are specially engaged during a great part of the year in fishing for plaice and other flat fishes, which are usually exported frozen to the European markets. So while cod and herring are the most important of the food fishes, one by one others are finding place in the economy. Among the kinds sought are haddock, Norway haddock, saithe and prawns. There is some whaling.

Part of the fish utilization is the production of medicinal oils in factories ashore and on board trawlers; there are fish-meal factories both on ship and ashore.

The importance of the fisheries to Iceland is indicated by the fact that marine products now form about 80% of total exports. It is therefore economically important for Iceland to acquire a scientific understanding of the biology of the food fishes, their habits, their yearly or other fluctuations. These studies are carried out in the School of Applied Science in Reykjavik.

Iceland is a member of the International Council for the Exploration of the Sea.

CHAPTER X

Other Industries

Ít is well known that an industry based on a home market cannot pay its way until a concentrated market is developed—that is until towns come into being. So there was little but home industry in Iceland down to the end of the last century.

In earlier times home industry was common. Worsteds, homespuns, knitted goods and yarn were then the chief exports. Raw wool was not exported until the latter half of the seventeenth century. Woolen and homespun cloth, together with butter and tallow, were used within the country to barter for marine produce.

The Danish trade monopoly was, of course, a blight on native industries as on most other things. In the free trade era following 1854 the prices of Icelandic wool rose considerably. In the chapter on the co-operative movement we mentioned that live sheep were at one time sent to England. The farmers were paid in gold and money transactions began to take the place of barter. Foreign textiles dropped in price and became more easily obtainable. The fisheries gained in strength and importance; people began to move from rural districts into towns and cities. In addition, many emigrated to the United States and Canada. All these factors led to the decline of home industry. It has not ceased entirely but its products are no longer on the market.

Trades and handicrafts had flourished in neighboring countries for almost a century before Iceland began considering them an independent occupation. Along with the growth of the towns the handicrafts have been increasing. Trade restrictions and protective tariffs all over the world have hastened this development. It is estimated that the percentage of those who earned their living by industry and handicraft increased from 1.1 in 1861 to 14.4 in 1930. Since 1930 the proportion has been rising fast. Statistics for the three decades beginning 1910 (in terms of total population) show:

	1910	1920	1930
Reykjavik	22.5	30.6	28.8
Other towns	13.9	21.1	20.7
Trading centers	13.9	13.7	16.7
Rural districts	2.1	2.5	3.4

Down to 1930 no external causes stimulated the growth of industry; nor were special efforts made to increase it. Its development automatically followed the changes in methods of production and in modes of life. This is shown clearly by the development and prosperity of the different branches of industry.

In the period 1910–30 the number of those who

lived by building of whatever description (except carpentry) increased more than tenfold; the number of carpenters was doubled; the technical and chemical industries which were hardly known in 1910 had become important by 1930; the food industry, in 1910 mainly in the hands of bakers, increased more than five times; the metal industry trebled; printing and book manufacture nearly doubled. The lowest rate of increase was in the market where home industry was still a factor—weaving, cloth manufacture, and ready-to-wear clothing.

Since the beginning of the world depression, about 1929, the shortage of foreign credits has compelled the government to restrict importation of goods which can easily be done without, and to forbid the import of many nonessentials. A study of the problem has shown that requirements can often be filled at home and restrictions are, of course, most rigorous on such articles.

The young and growing industry in Iceland is therefore a result of the necessity to find some new possibilities of production which will save foreign credits. The chief means towards this end is the greater utilization of native raw materials, importation of raw materials or partly finished articles instead of fully finished goods and their manufacture in the country for the home market. That more new industries have not already been established is mainly for want of capital and because of tariff restrictions. Some steps have been taken to change these inhibiting conditions.

Customs duties are imposed as a means of revenue for

the government and not as a protection for home products. In 1931 an act was passed providing rebate of such duties on materials for industrial enterprises in cases where competitive foreign articles carried no import duty or less duty than that of the raw material. The whole of the customs legislation is now being revised.

In the interests of capital, in 1935 an act was passed which referred to new industries. Those which manufactured goods not heretofore manufactured in the country, and those which used new methods or materials, were exempted from state and municipal taxes for three years. There is no excise duty on any industrial product now except on such luxuries as confectionery, beer and mineral water.

Also in 1935 was passed an Act Concerning the Establishment of a Separate Fund for Loans to Industrial Enterprises.

Along the lines of expansion of present industries much can be done in the fisheries. For instance, cod-liver oil is commonly exported in a non-destearinated state. Destearination at home, however, began in 1933. Herring oil is still exported in a crude state but refined fish oil is used in the country in the manufacture of soap and margarine. It would be most natural to refine Icelandic fish oil at home—for a minimum, what is needed for home use. The possibilities have been examined; but nothing has been done, mainly because sufficient electric power is not available in the chief herring stations. However, a new electric plant now in construction near one of the large herring centers may bring about this development.

Down to recent years there has been very little industrial activity connected with agricultural produce though, as we have said in the chapter on the co-operative movement, mutton is being exported frozen. In 1936 only one third of the meat exported was salted, against some nine tenths in 1928. The greater part of the agricultural exports are unmanufactured. In 1936 only 0.9% of the value of the whole exports was in finished goods.

Since the end of the last century there have been woolen mills in the country which supply the home market. There are at present three; their production has nearly doubled in the last ten years.

Formerly most skins not used at home were exported raw. Now the tanning industry is on the increase. In 1937 about 87% more skins were tanned in the country than in 1933.

The milk industry is also increasing rapidly. Some of the largest dairies produced around 8300 tons in 1937 against 500 tons in 1930. In addition, the canned milk industry now fully satisfies the home market whereas before 1932 considerable quantities were imported.

Of commodities manufactured chiefly from foreign materials we may mention margarine, crackers, beer, mineral waters, chicory and confectionery. The production of most of these is increasing rapidly. Margarine factories have been operating since 1920 but not until 1931 on a scale large enough to satisfy domestic needs.

During the period 1929–34 production increased by about 55% and margarine is now exported.

The manufacture of crackers, which was begun in 1927, nearly doubled the years 1933–37; the production of chocolate more than doubled; that of confectionery was increased five or six times. Brewery products, from a start in 1913, have decreased by some 50%. Mineral waters production (begun in 1905) has more than doubled in the years 1932–37.

In the clothing industry manufactures from foreign materials include oilskins, working clothes, shirts, caps, ties, shoes and gloves. In the leather goods industry a start has been made with native skins. All these have begun since 1928; most of them within the last year or two.

A start was made in 1922 for the production of such things as shoe polish, metal polish, wax polish, soap and various toilet articles. There is growth in quantity and in variety.

Foreign raw materials are used in the shipbuilding industry. No iron ships have as yet been built in the country and most repairs to them have had to be made abroad. Now it is possible to have repairs made at Reykjavik for ships up to 1000 tons. It is proposed to expand the shipyard to accommodate ships up to 4000 tons, and possibly to build some. Wooden ships are usually built at home, and also repaired, but the materials have to be imported for lack of suitable timber.

Mechanical ironwork has made progress during late

Home industry has not ceased entirely but its products are no longer on the regular markets.

years. The center of the industry is Reykjavik. An impetus was given to this and similar enterprises which require a great deal of power when a new electric plant began operating in 1937. The old one, in use since 1921, had become too small; the new one has been built with a view of increased requirements over a long period. Electricity, both for industrial and home use, was therefore greatly reduced in price in 1937.

In spite of the progress of the iron industry, very little machinery is manufactured in the country. The need for it increases as each new enterprise is begun.

Growing up with the fisheries has been the production of such things as hemp, buoys, barrels, drums, boxes, tins, bottles and the like.

All building materials, except stone, gravel and sand, have to be imported. Nowadays reinforced concrete is most generally used. It is probable that cement may be produced in the country, but nothing has been done along this line so far. Cementware, pipes and the like have been manufactured since around the beginning of the century. Native insulating materials (dry turf, chopped peat, and more recently pumice) have been used to some extent. The pumice has been very satisfactory and experiments have been made in building small houses entirely of it. These houses are not yet old enough to furnish an index of durability. There are unlimited quantities of pumice and the industry is expected to develop.

The manufacture of paint goods was begun in 1936. Foreign raw materials are used exclusively.

All household utensils other than furniture have been imported. The furniture industry has increased a great deal during the last years. The manufacture of steel furniture has been established. Other new products are central heating radiators and musical instruments.

Mining is not an important industry because the country, geologically speaking, is young. The only coals are lignite and brown, which are not considered paying propositions in normal times. There is a considerable amount of Iceland spar and sulphur, both of which have been mined in the recent past. There are also various clays with commercial possibilities. It is considered that there are certain amounts of iron, gold and copper, but the practicability of mining them has not been fully investigated.

CHAPTER XI

Commerce

SOME of the first settlers of Iceland were traders. In spite of the more heralded piracy, a good proportion of the early seafarers were engaged in peaceful dealings with other countries. That situation lasted for about 300 years, with Icelanders transporting their own produce to European markets and bringing home cargoes of foreign goods; but in the thirteenth century, for reasons which we have explained, Icelandic shipping ceased to be of any considerable importance. Needed repairs were not made to her ships, replacements were neglected and she gradually became dependent on other nations. In the fourteenth and fifteenth centuries the trade was largely in the hands of English and of Hanseatic merchants, a condition which lasted until Denmark closed Iceland ports to all but Danish vessels.

The lifting of the trade barrier in 1854 caused no immediate revival of the nearly defunct trade. There were only fifty-eight business houses in the country, half of them operated by foreigners. In the revival which began in 1855 the interest of the Icelanders was at first mainly in home trade, and maritime affairs were left in foreign hands. This began to change about 1900 with the establishment of Icelandic wholesale houses and agencies. By 1912 there were fifteen; in 1936 there were eighty.

Between 1854 and 1900 business houses had increased from fifty-eight to 208, of which fifty were foreign-owned; by 1936 there were 1124 firms registered, of which only three were foreign.

Depending on their nature, business houses belong to the Icelandic Chamber of Commerce or to the Federation of Icelandic Co-operative Societies, both of which have their headquarters in Reykjavik. The rest are state monopolies (wines and spirits, tobaccos, etc.) and are run on wholesale lines as a source of income for the Treasury.

State monopolies were created during the latter stages of the Great War when world conditions made trade difficult. The state then undertook purchase in the foreign market of some of the most indispensable necessities, which were then resold to merchants and co-operatives alike. This resulted in government stores or *Landsverzlun*, which during the last years of their existence traded only in tobacco and petroleum. The state monopoly of these two products, established in 1922 and 1923 and placed under the Landsverzlun, ceased in 1925. Thereafter petroleum was sold by the state in competition with other dealers. In 1927 the Landsverzlun was abolished except for the State Liquor Monopoly which was established in 1922 and has the exclusive right to import all wines and spirits. Still more recently, there have been created other monopolies, each with the sole right of importing goods within its sphere of activity—as, for example, fertilizers.

In 1930, when the Icelandic State Broadcasting Service was established, the state took over the sale of receiving sets. In 1931 the monopoly on tobacco was revived, to which in 1935 were added matches and cigarette paper. The same year a state monopoly was created for all sorts of electrical machinery, electrical apparatus and installation material, automobiles, trucks, parts and accessories and tree seedlings. The monopoly on intoxicants has also been extended to include perfumes, essences and compressed yeast.

Moreover, the Union of Icelandic Fish Producers has been granted the sole right of exporting salt fish.

In 1917 the merchants of Iceland established the *Verzlunarrád Íslands* (Iceland's Chamber of Commerce) with headquarters in Reykjavik, to act on their behalf abroad. It issues a *Commercial Gazette* monthly and has set up a court of arbitration in commercial and shipping affairs.

In percentage rapidity of growth the development of commerce in Iceland has had few parallels. At the beginning of the present century the nation was poor and its methods of production were primitive. Appendix E, Table 2, traces a growth from total exports of $2,605,800 in the five-year period 1901–05 to $12,410,500 for the single year 1936. In 1914 the index number of imports was 100, in 1936 it was 220; for exports the figures are 100 and 207 respectively.

Such an increase would be impossible without a corresponding development in banking institutions and means of communication. The National Bank of Iceland was established in 1885. At present there are two others, The Fishing Trade Bank of Iceland, and the Farmers' Bank of Iceland. Notes in circulation amounted to $818,250 in 1915 and to $3,017,500 in 1937. In 1918 savings and other deposits totaled $9,211,250 and in 1937 $15,889,-000.

Table 1 (Appendix E) shows that during the period 1900–37 the trade balance with foreign countries was on the whole favorable; the price received for exports has paid for the goods imported. This is a necessary condition, for Iceland must pay in Europe for such things as amortization of foreign loans as well.

Inherent in the situation is a change in the ratios of imports and exports. As will be seen from Table 2, exports are mainly the products of the fisheries and of agriculture. The increase in exports may be mainly traced to the increased capacity of the fishing fleet, a development which reached its peak in 1932 when marine products accounted for 92.1% of the value of exported goods. The chief agricultural products are meat, wool, hides and furs. As previously mentioned, until about ten years ago all of the meat for export was salted, while now more than half is shipped frozen. This development was subsidized by the state which established refrigerating plants. Table 3 of Appendix E shows the chief goods exported in the year 1937.

Appendix E is deceptive in that its percentages imply that agricultural development has not kept pace with that of the fisheries. We have discussed the agricultural situation in an earlier chapter and here merely point out that the increased production has to a great extent been absorbed within the country itself.

In a bid for wider markets for her goods Iceland has placed first the quality of her products, backed by rigid standards and by inspecting and grading laws.

Imports have been changing in kind. It is difficult to show these changes for they are of great variety, but some idea may be gleaned from Table 4, which shows periodic fluctuations of such things as food, luxuries, etc. For example, food imports were 18.6% in 1913 but only 10% in the period 1931–35, whereas the figures for building materials are 6.5% and 9.9% respectively.

Also continually changing is the ratio between goods for production (capital goods) and those for consumption, as shown in Table 5. Briefly, the proportion in the period 1916–20 was 46.8% consumers' goods, 53.2% capital goods, while in the year 1936 the figures were 31.1% and 68.9% respectively. This increase in capital goods and decrease in consumers' goods is a natural result of the change which is taking place in the occupational life of the country. As we have seen in the chapter "Other Industries," more goods for consumption are now being produced at home. Another factor is the restrictions on certain imports which have changed classifications drastically. These are analyzed in Table 6 which shows the division of goods classes in 1937.

As we have said, right down to the beginning of the present century the Icelanders were dependent upon one or two other nations for the whole of their foreign trade. When the country was able to resume control the situation changed. Goods were sent to more and more countries. Things were now sold direct to the lands of consumption; imports were bought direct, without the intervention of foreign middlemen. In 1900, for instance, 90% of the imports came from Denmark and Great Britain and 66% of the exports went to these countries. Table 7 shows the greater diffusion of commerce from the time of the World War to 1937. The huge increase in Iceland's trade with the United States in 1918 is explained by the fact that the war had disrupted shipping. In the years following the armistice the steamship lines returned to the Old World routes and Iceland's trade with the New World declined. However, if regular sailings are re-established from Iceland to the United States and Canada the probabilities are that trade will increase far beyond even 1918.

An analysis of trade relations shows, that while Iceland is a heavy consumer of goods made in Great Britain, Denmark, Germany and Norway, these countries do not buy proportionate amounts from her. On the other hand, Spain, Italy and Portugal, from which Iceland buys very

Dried fish is an important factor in Icelandic trade.

little, are the largest consumers of Icelandic klipfish. For example, in 1933, 80.7% of imports came from Great Britain, Denmark, Germany and Norway; while only 36.2% of exports went to these countries. Thus Iceland had an unfavorable trade balance of $5,772,500. During the same year 55.4% of Icelandic exports went to Spain, Italy and Portugal; but Iceland bought only 5% of her imports from them, a favorable trade balance of $6,850,-000.

While world trade was free and the policy of restrictions had not been widely adopted this unequal division did not matter; for the surplus obtained from the Mediterranean trade covered the deficit created in the more northerly countries. But in 1934 Spain restricted the importation of klipfish and demanded a trade agreement with Iceland. Italy followed suit the next year and caused a further shrinkage of the market for Iceland's chief export article. The civil war in Spain stopped practically all trade with that country. The results may be seen in Table 7. From an export to Spain of 28.8% in 1933, the figure in 1937 had dropped to 1%. Exports to Italy fell from 12.3% to 5%.

Iceland naturally did all she could to counteract this severe dislocation of world markets. She could no longer afford to buy so many imports, so emphasis had to be placed on more varied production within the country. At the same time, production was increased where goods had a world market. The capacity of the herring factories, for instance, was expanded from 2,738,000 pounds per

24 hours in 1934 to 8,037,000 pounds per 24 hours in 1937. The value of herring exports increased from $2,000,-000 in 1933 to $4,975,000 in 1937. With these and other measures, restriction on currency and imports were. imposed to balance trade. The results are apparent in Table 7. The unfavorable trade balance with the countries from which goods are chiefly bought was reduced from $5,-772,500 to $750,000 in 1937. Imports from these countries were reduced from 80.7% to 60% and exports increased from 36.2% to 57%.

The foreign trade to Iceland is, in percentages, heavy; for the country produces and exports large quantities of comparatively few articles and must buy numerous kinds of merchandise that she cannot produce herself. For this reason the foreign trade, when you take the total population into account, is greater than that of most other nations. In 1937 the total imports and exports amounted to $26,650,000, or about $230 per capita. By way of comparison, the foreign trade of Great Britain in 1936 was $170 per capita and that of the United States about $41.50.

Imported goods are treated under two classifications: first, as to whether they are goods for production or goods for consumption; second, as to the state of their manufacture. In 1936 goods for production accounted for 79% of the total imports and goods for consumption 21%. Of the total imports 50% were fully finished goods, 29% slightly manufactured and 21% raw materials. The classification of exports shows the opposite trend. Goods for consumption amounted to 63%, for production 37%. Of the total exports 69% were raw materials, 30% partly finished goods and slightly less than 1% fully finished. From the point of view of other countries and their businessmen, the trade with Iceland is thus shown to be specially advantageous.

CHAPTER XII

Communications

SHIPS AND SHIPPING of necessity play a large part in the affairs of an island country. Throughout the time of the commonwealth (930–1261) there were frequent sailings from Norway and the British Isles. Many of the settlers were shipowners; many had been the type of buccaneers called vikings. Their seafaring skill and equipment stood them in good stead; for in the colonization of the country various things (among them timber) had to be brought in from abroad.

The vessels of the colonization period and of the republic were of varied types and sizes. The fourteen which were used in 986 for the establishment of the first Icelandic colony in Greenland have been much commented upon and were perhaps average, or somewhat below it. They are considered to have carried an average of thirty people each, together with their household goods and their stock of the domestic animals, among which horses, cattle and sheep were chief, although pigs and fowl were included.

An average length for ships of the republic, say around 1000, is considered to have been 100 feet, the extreme length being 160 feet, but that would be only for "long-ships," craft designed for battle. The trading ships, which were shorter, with a higher freeboard, and which were stronger and more seaworthy than the warships, are believed to have carried between countries cargoes averaging around fifteen tons. They were fully loaded when they were three fifths below water at their middle. Many judges consider (as, for instance, William Hovgaard, Professor of Naval Design at the Massachusetts Institute of Technology) that they sailed faster and were safer in bad weather than ships of the time of Columbus.

Most of the sailings from Iceland to neighbor countries during the republic were in the early summer when European vessels came to trade and domestic vessels called at foreign ports for the same purpose. It is interesting to remember, then, that the first definitely recorded voyagers to Iceland left Ireland in February, 795 A.D. and returned to Ireland in August.

On arrival in Iceland the goods of foreign merchants were brought ashore and exchanged for Icelandic produce; but, as there were no shops and as some of the payments could not be made until the following spring, the traders usually could not return home the same summer. So they put up their vessels, stayed the winter and in this way became much better acquainted with the people than would otherwise be the case. We find many references to them in the old Icelandic sagas. Not a few relished their first winter so much that they remained as immigrants.

Down to about the year 1000 the Icelanders owned enough ships to provide suitable trade and communication with other countries. During the eleventh century the number of vessels began to decline and trade slipped more and more from home control. After 1200 most of the traders, captains and shipowners recorded in connection with sailings were foreigners. At this time there was little direct communication with any country other than Norway and passage was mainly on Norwegian boats. For that reason Icelanders now had to go to Norway first, no matter how roundabout such a route might be for their eventual destination.

During the years 1261–64 when Iceland came under the supremacy of Norway, the king was in charge of trade. An agreement was signed which stipulated that six ships a year should call in Iceland. Norwegian ships thereafter continued to be the main source of communication until about the beginning of the fifteenth century when the English, and later the Germans, came in to trade. They gave Norway such competition that it was no longer profitable for the Norwegians to maintain regular schedules and sailings became erratic. The non-Scandinavian trade continued until Denmark closed the country in 1602.

In the years 1602–1787 trade was restricted to a few Danish concessionaires; then it was made free to all Danish subjects. Finally (as often repeated) Iceland was opened to foreign vessels in 1854 and trade became free.

In spite of all the restrictions—and the Danes kept a watchful eye on the country—there is evidence that sporadic non-Scandinavian trade persisted during the closed period. Shortly after 1600 the Spaniards began to come in, mainly for whales. With these there were trade relations, though they were not on the whole satisfactory, until the news reached the king. He then decreed that any Spaniard caught in the country should be put to death.

During the seventeenth century covert trade was carried on with English fishermen who not only brought goods into Iceland but also carried Icelanders to England in connection with the trading. There was trade with the Dutch as well—whereupon came a royal decree forbidding anyone to land people from English or Dutch vessels under penalty of confiscation of property.

We also know of sailings from Hamburg down to the third decade of the nineteenth century. Furthermore, one Icelander, Bjarni Sivertsen, was enterprising enough to build a fleet of ten ships which he used for coastwise and ocean freighting. His ships went to Denmark, Scotland, France and Spain. During the war between England and Denmark (1808–09) several English ships came to Iceland and the Danes could barely maintain their trade.

When the monopoly was lifted the merchants trading in Iceland took over the shipping. There was, too, an enterprising group of farmers in the north who formed a trading company, *Gránufélag*. They owned one cargo vessel in 1870 and later added two others. During the period 1877–83 these three ships maintained regular sailings.

The present shipping is an outgrowth of several factors. Of the three companies now operating one is Danish, one Norwegian and one Icelandic.

The United Shipping Company of Copenhagen began a service in 1866 with the ships Arcturus, Anglo-Dane and Phoenix. This was continued until 1870 when the Danish government assumed control and employed the SS Diana. During the years 1876–79 United again maintained service, in co-operation with the Danish government, though from 1880 to 1914 little was carried beyond passengers and mail. At present this company has a sailing every three weeks from Copenhagen in the Dronning Alexandrine. The ship stops at the Faroes both on the outward and homeward voyage.

The Bergenske Steamship Company of Bergen sent its first ship, the cargo boat Uranus, in 1908. In 1909 they operated the SS Flora which had passenger accommodation. In 1913–14 this company made an agreement with the Icelandic government that they would have two ships on the Iceland–Norway run, and the SS Pollux was added. Both of these ships were sunk during the war. The company then suspended sailings until 1919 when they resumed service with one cargo boat, the SS Lyra which calls at Faroes and Iceland fortnightly. Another vessel has maintained service from Oslo and Bergen to the east and north coasts of Iceland and to Reykjavik since 1925.

At the end of the nineteenth and the beginning of the twentieth century, one man played a large part in the development of Icelandic shipping. Thor E. Tulinius, a wholesale merchant of Copenhagen, carried on a brisk trade with Iceland. He owned many tramp steamers and chartered others. At the turn of the century he wanted to start a passenger service and through his initiative the Thore Steamship Company was founded in 1903. He was the largest shareholder and managing director. This company acquired the ships Perwie and Mjölnir, and later the Kong Inge, Scotland, Kong Tryggve, Kong Helge, Ingolf and Sterling, all of which sailed between Iceland and Europe. In addition, the company maintained a costal service with the ships Austri, Vestri and Perwie. The company was run with great enterprise and flourished for a while; but in 1913 financial difficulties compelled it to suspend operations. However, through Tulinius and the Thore Company, the Icelanders had learned to understand that what they really needed was a service of their own.

Several patriotic and energetic Icelanders thereupon began a campaign to awaken interest in a domestic company. On January 17, 1914, the Iceland Steamship Company was established, with headquarters in Reykjavik and a branch in Copenhagen.

The company's first ship, Gullfoss, arrived in Reykjavik on April 15, 1915. In June of the same year the company acquired another ship, the older Godafoss. Sailings at first were to Scotland and Denmark; but when the Great War interfered they were sent direct to New York. Unfortunately for the company the SS Godafoss was wrecked; but it was soon replaced and the Lagarfoss and Gullfoss plied the route between Iceland and North America.

After the war the Iceland Steamship Company had a third boat built, the new Godafoss. Sailings to New York were discontinued, and the old routes were resumed. In 1926 regular service to Hamburg was begun, and later to Antwerp. The connection with the United States is partly maintained, however; for the company handles via British or continental ports most of the goods bought and sold in America by Icelanders.

The Iceland Steamship Company now has a regular service to Great Britain, Denmark, Germany and Belgium; also, their boats often make calls at Dutch, Norwegian and Swedish ports. The company further maintains an extensive coastwise service in Iceland, although they have no special ship for this purpose—they use around the coast the vessels of their foreign service.

The board of directors of the Steamship Company consists of nine members, one of whom is appointed by the government while two are elected by American Icelanders who are important shareholders. It now has six vessels, Gullfoss, 1414 gross reg. tons; Godafoss, 1542 g.r.t.; Bruarfoss, 1579 g.r.t.; Dettifoss, 1604 g.r.t.; Lagarfoss, 1211 g.r.t.; Selfoss, 775 g.r.t. All of these except the cargo boat Selfoss are combination passenger-and-cargo boats.

The passenger accommodation on these ships is modern. The cargo business is also modern, for some of the boats are equipped with freezing plants. The size of the ships is considered convenient for their present routes. However, the company is preparing to build a new boat which will be larger and faster and will be specially designed for passenger service.

The average speed of the Icelandic company's vessels is about twelve to thirteen knots, covering the distance from the Westman Islands (last port of call in Iceland) to Leith (the port of Edinburgh), Scotland, in three days, and Westman Islands to Copenhagen in four days. The main routes are to Copenhagen, calling at Leith, and to Hamburg, calling at Hull.

In 1937 these boats carried 3313 passengers between countries and 10,243 coastwise. During the same year the ships carried 92,000 tons of freight between countries and 11,000 coastwise.

The establishment of the Iceland Steamship Company was both opportune and fortunate. The history of past centuries had shown how unsafe it was to trust another nation with shipping matters; without her own domestic service it is doubtful whether Iceland could have secured necessities during the Great War.

All goods are not yet brought to Iceland by Icelandic boats, but several steamship companies have been founded with freighting as their object.

The Reykjavik Steamship Company, Ltd., founded in 1932, operates two boats, the SS Hekla, 1450 tons, and the SS Katla, 1680 tons. Both of these have been sailing to Mediterranean countries, to Great Britain and northern Europe. They have also sailed to America.

The Isafold Steamship Company, founded in 1933, owns one boat, the Edda, 2050 tons, which is used on a Mediterranean service.

The Skallagrimur Steamship Company, of Borgarnes, in southwest Iceland, owns the MS Laxfoss, which maintains regular service between Reykjavik and Borgarnes. In summer and autumn sailings are every day; in winter two or three times a week.

The Akureyri Co-operative Society has carried on considerable transport of goods. In 1934 they bought the SS Snaefell, 1000 gross tons, and this boat has since 1935 made each year seven to ten voyages between Iceland and other countries fully laden with goods. In 1937 they bought the SS Hvassafell, 221 gross tons, which is used both to catch herring and to transport frozen fish to market.

As an emergency measure because of the war, the government in 1917 bought three boats, the SS Sterling for coastal service, the SS Willemoes and the SS Borg for ocean freighting. The Sterling was stranded in 1923, and the Borg was sold the same year. A new boat, SS Esja, replaced the Sterling, and in 1927 she was the only boat owned by the government. (The Willemoes had been sold to the Iceland Steamship Company and renamed Selfoss.) In 1930 the government established its own shipping office for the Esja and bought the Sudin for coastal service. The Esja was used for passenger service between Reykjavik and Glasgow, but has now been sold to Chile. She will be replaced by a new and larger ship.

There are no railways in Iceland and it is unlikely that they will ever be built, for motorbus and airplane are making them unnecessary.

The first motorcars were brought to Iceland in 1913. Their number has increased so rapidly that there are now more than a thousand engaged in goods transport, with nearly that many for passengers. Most of these vehicles are registered in Reykjavik. A regular service is kept up between the various parts of the country, though in winter it is largely suspended owing to the heavy fall of snow in the mountains. There are at present twenty-nine fixed bus routes.

Between Reykjavik and Akureyri two types of services are maintained: "Regular," all the way by bus, requiring about two 12-hour days; "Express," by boat from Reykjavik to Borgarnes and thence by bus to Akureyri. This takes from fifteen to seventeen hours.

From about June 1 to October 1 there is a bus each way between Akureyri and Reykjavik daily. On three days a week the express buses operate, four days a week the regular buses.

The bus season may not open as early as June 1 but may extend well past October 1. Then all through traffic ceases for the winter on the full Reykjavik–Akureyri line, although parts of the route continue open locally.

The total cost is about $10.00–the regular bus charges a little more than the express; and there are the night's lodging and extra meals. On express buses the fare is $6.75 plus two or three meals; total cost about $8.75.

Each bus has a seating capacity of from eighteen to twenty-one. The law requires a second bus if there is one more passenger than seats on any day. Passenger buses also carry baggage and mail, but freight goes by truck.

In spite of an aggressive road-making program during the last decades there is not yet a nearly satisfactory network. Concern for aviation is therefore strong.

In 1919 and 1920 some experiments were made with a small-sized plane. In 1928 *Flugfélag Islands* (The Aeronautical Society of Iceland) was founded and operated for four years. A four-passenger plane was hired for transport between Reykjavik and various places on the coast. During the summer 16,160 miles were covered and 500 passengers carried. The following spring two four-passenger seaplanes were hired; 34,900 miles were flown and 1100 passengers were carried. In the next two years the mileages increased; but the number of passengers diminished, because greater emphasis was put upon long-distance flying. In 1929–31 one of the seaplanes was engaged during the herring season to locate herring shoals and report them to the fishing fleet. To meet this expense a small tax was imposed on the herring boats. A bad season, with resulting complaints from the fishermen, caused the withdrawal of the tax. Without this support the Flugfélag could not meet operating expenses and it went out of business.

The summer of 1938 *Flugfélag Akureyrar* (Aeronautical Society of Akureyri) was organized for the purpose of summer flying in a five-seater Waco which was named the Eagle. Although this Society has a regular route—Reykjavik–Siglufjördur–Akureyri—it is a taxi service as well and will fly to any point where there is business. Operations showed such a profit that the Society decided to continue its flights into the winter. The following account is translated from the Reykjavik newspaper *Morgunbladid*, December 15, 1938:

THE EAGLE TO FLY IN WINTER

Flugfélag Akureyrar has decided to continue flying throughout the winter.

At one time it was doubted whether the company would be able to maintain a winter service, this having been considered more likely to be an unprofitable season financially. The days are shorter and fewer people travel.

It is reported that the government refused to guarantee losses on this operation. . . .

Now the company has decided to continue winter flying in spite of the lack of government guarantee. They will fly both to Akureyri and to Siglufjördur, but only according to both weather and traffic demand. They will probably fly to Isafjördur once a week and to Borgarnes twice a week, and perhaps elsewhere according to demand. For instance,

the Eagle flew yesterday with a load of mail for Stykkisholm
and Budardal and made a circuit of the whole district.

In general it is contemplated that the Postal Department
will make considerable use of the airplane, amounting thus
to a degree of subsidy. Indeed, it will be of the greatest con-
venience to the Post Office to be able to make use of this
service, especially when other transportation methods are so
inadequate as they are here in winter.

Altogether the Eagle carried last summer 750 passengers
a total distance of more than 31,000 passenger miles. The total number of separate flights was 358. The plane completed
successfully 99.3% of all work attempted. . . . From Reykjavik there were 60 flights to Akureyri, 61 to Siglufjördur.

The company did operate throughout the winter of
1938–39. Their success, and that of planes owned by
private individuals, is of great importance to Iceland, for
it assures a dependable service that can reach even the
most out-of-the-way towns and farms in that winter
period when mountain roads are closed to bus and car.

We have said that roads are still rough and crude in
many parts. Jolting over them might seriously aggravate
the troubles of a person needing an operation. Airplanes
fly smoothly; they do not jolt a patient seriously. For
this reason doctors order hospitalization when an airplane is available although they would not order it if the
conveyance had to be over a rough mountain highway;
or, scarcely better, if it were by a coastal boat, for these
small craft tumble about in the rough seas, jolting the
patient and likely making him seasick.

Not merely do patients come to hospitals now by plane; they are able to return by plane from the hospital to their homes days and even weeks earlier than a doctor would have permitted transport by road or coastal ship.

Failing an airplane, it is in serious cases the doctor rather than the patient who has to travel. He makes his way on horseback or by skis to the farmhouse and sometimes operates—as in American pioneering days—on the kitchen table. Such operations cannot have a good percentage of success; for not merely are work conditions unfavorable but the operation has to be done by a local man, who is not necessarily a competent surgeon. A plane takes any serious case to the best hospital in Iceland, or at any rate to the best in that part of the country.

The obvious strategic position of Iceland for the operation of a line across the northerly Atlantic has been discounted hitherto by foreign lands, and even by the aeronautically little-informed Icelanders themselves, on the supposition that the Icelandic climate was hostile to flying. Now, particularly under the stress of mercy flights, Iceland has seen this "stock model" American plane operating in some of their worst weather, always with greater success than could have been attained by any other transport and never with harm to itself, to passenger or to pilot. This gives renewed confidence that aviation will eventually utilize the strategic position of Iceland just as completely as if it were a tropical or subtropical island, like the Hawaiis or the Azores.

Icelanders like to think of the airways of the future

in relation to the seaways of the past. The country was a steppingstone in the European discovery of America. They were themselves a seafaring nation of consequence and took the lead in westward discovery and colonization a thousand years ago. Things are now on such a different scale that Icelanders cannot be leaders where vast aviation capital is required, but they can nevertheless feel satisfaction in that they are to be a link in that prospective air commerce which, for them at least, takes the place of the viking navigations between the continents a thousand years ago.

There have been many flights across the North Atlantic by way of Iceland and Greenland, exploring tentatively this intercontinental highway of the future. There was a first-flight interest in the visit of the U.S. army round-the-world planes in 1924. There was perhaps greatest significance in the flight of Colonel and Mrs Charles A. Lindbergh in 1933. For the Lindberghs came prospecting a route for an American company that has broad geographic scope, that operates scheduled services throughout the year not only in South America and Alaska but across the Pacific and (as planned for 1939) across the middle Atlantic—Pan-American Airways. Like most of their predecessors and successors, the Lindberghs navigated easily the portions of the route which had been considered most dangerous, those over Greenland and Iceland.

The Lindberghs differed from some other flyers who have visited Iceland in being successful on their whole circuit (from New York by way of Labrador, Baffin

Island, Greenland, Iceland and the Scandinavian countries to the Soviet Union, and then back by way of Spain, North Africa and South America). So there have been no misunderstandings resulting from that air voyage. Other flights by way of Iceland have been misunderstood; through those misunderstandings they have created the feeling that the vicinity of Iceland had been shown to be dangerous. An example was the flight of the American, Parker Cramer, and the Canadian, Oliver Pacquette, in 1931.

Cramer-Pacquette flew without incident across Labrador, Greenland, Iceland and the Faroe Islands to the Shetlands. They took off safely from the Shetlands—and were lost in the North Sea between Scotland and Denmark. So their tragedy really occurred in waters that were being flown over repeatedly even then; but because the flight had been through the supposedly difficult "Far North" their deaths have been more frequently blamed upon Greenland and Iceland than upon the British and Danish territories between which they actually were lost.

It is through such reasons for clarifying an international picture that Icelanders take more than local satisfaction in the ease and safety with which planes have operated both throughout the summer of 1938 and (without de-icers or other special trappings) the winter of 1938–39.

Postal service in Iceland has always been under state management. Until quite recently all mail was conveyed

either by sea or on horseback, but in the course of the
last few years motorbuses have replaced other convey-
ances on the chief mail roads. The horse caravan is seen

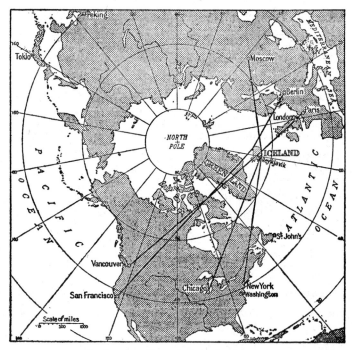

Iceland and some future airways.

now only in out-of-the-way places, and on roads which
are not passable by bus the year round. In 1935 there
were 533 permanent post offices and sub-post offices
which carried 1,804,000 letters and post cards, 1,564,000
newspaper packets and other printed matter and 376,000
parcels. Later figures are not available but decreased

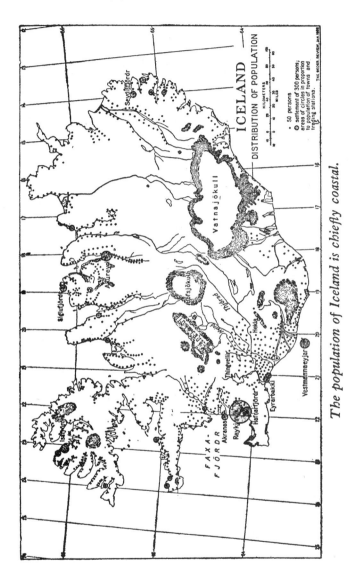

ICELAND

DISTRIBUTION OF POPULATION

KILOMETERS

MILES

• 50 persons
◉ settlement of 300 persons;
  areas of circles in proportion
  to population of towns and
  fishing stations.   THE GEOGR. REVIEW, JAN. 1925

Seyðisfjörðr

Vatnajökull

Akureyri

Siglufjörðr

Hofsjökull

Mýrdalsjökull

Thingvellir

Hekla

Heidá

Reykjir

Hafnarfjörðr

Eyrarbakki

Vestmannaeyjar

Ísafjörðr

Akranes

FAXA-
FJÖRÐR

The population of Iceland is chiefly coastal.

amounts are unlikely. It is probable that there were increases.

In 1906 a submarine cable was laid from the Shetland Islands through the Faroes to Seydisfjördur on the east coast. *Det store nordiske Telegrafselskab* (The Great Northern Telegraph Company) in Denmark laid the cable, with grants from the Icelandic and Danish treasuries, and was given sole operating rights for twenty years. This contract was renewed in 1926.

When the cable was laid there were no telegraphs or telephones in the country, except the Reykjavik local exchange and a line between Hafnarfjördur and Reykjavik; but a telegraph line was constructed from Seydisfjördur to Reykjavik and telephone lines are steadily being added. All trunk lines are constructed by the state, the local lines partly at the expense of the districts through which they run.

In August 1935 radio service was established between Iceland and Europe. Communication with the United States, at first via Great Britain, was made direct in 1938.

When telegraphic connection was first established and weather reports were sent out daily Iceland became one of the most important meteorological centers. Bad weather, cyclones and depressions coming from the west were usually first discovered around Iceland. Since the advent of radio, people living in Great Britain, Germany and the Scandinavian countries are used to reports beginning: "A depression at the south coast of Iceland," or "Bad weather approaching from Iceland." The English joke about it in their comic strips, even in verse. One poem exhorts Iceland to stop exporting cyclones—to send eiderdown instead.

The Meteorological Institute in Reykjavik now gathers information on weather conditions in various parts of Iceland and from foreign stations. Weather reports are then sent to all the principal telegraph offices in the country; twenty-four hour weather forecasts are broadcast (in Icelandic, English and German) two or three times a day. These are of value not only to the fishing fleet but to ships of every type and of many nations which ply the northern Atlantic.

CHAPTER XIII

Iceland for Tourists

LORD BRYCE, writing in 1923, recommends that only two kinds of people should visit Iceland, those who are interested in Scandinavian history and literature, and those "who belong to that happy and youthful class which enjoys a rough life for its own sake." Icelanders think his classification too exclusive; for experience has shown that, in order to enjoy himself thoroughly, the tourist need bring only one quality with him, that of desiring to venture off the beaten track. Roads, hotels and many other things have changed since Lord Bryce visited Iceland, but the land can still provide new and varied enchantments.

As we described in the chapter on communications, Iceland is reached from Copenhagen by the United Steamship Line, from Bergen by the Bergenske Steamship Line, and from Edinburgh (Leith), Hull, Copenhagen and Hamburg by the Iceland Steamship Line. In addition there is a government service between Reykjavik and Glasgow fortnightly during the summer.

First-class fare is about $32.50 (£6, 10s), with a slight reduction for round-trip tickets. Meals are $2.00 a day in addition. The trip from Hull takes about four days and less than that from the Scottish ports. During the summer the sea is usually calm, the voyage is refreshing and many find that the smallish boats have a charm of their own.

Charm or not, discomforts of overcrowding may and usually do occur on the voyages between May and September, particularly those from Leith, Scotland and Hull, England. But only late bookers suffer.

The last regular berth is perhaps disposed of soon after the holidays of the previous winter. Thereafter people who demand bookings, even after they have been warned of the overcrowding, will be taken on. A few of these are accommodated by sharing cabins with officers of the vessel. Others take passage knowing that they will have to sleep on benches in the smoking room, or in some other improvised location. There have been cases, after the pre-emption of all such spots, when groups of travelers as, for instance, an enthusiastic band of English university people, will insist on being taken as campers down in the hold on top of the cargo. These are such as Bryce had in mind, himself a university man and young in 1872, when he defined as one of the two kinds of travelers safe in cultivating Iceland those "who belong to that happy and youthful class which enjoys a rough life for its own sake."

Information about rates and sailings may be obtained ·

from any of the above companies, or from Statourist (State Tourist Information Bureau), Reykjavik. This bureau was established in 1936 to look after the interests of visitors—to see that they were charged moderate rates and to supply them with accurate information. Letters of inquiry addressed to Statourist get prompt replies.

With English for a language you get along fairly well in Iceland. In the larger towns at least one in four, man or woman, can understand you, and many will reply fluently—some in British English which they have learned in Europe, some in American English which they have brought home from the United States or Canada and still others in a sort of composite British-American English which they learn in school. You will find books in English at many farmhouses—which does not say that the family could talk with you, for the self-taught have less notion of the sounds than of the meanings of words.

Of the foreign languages which are helpful the best will be the Scandinavian tongues, Danish, Norwegian and Swedish, which between them are spoken by perhaps twice as many as English. German probably comes next after English, with French occasional.

After stating the obvious, that the language of Iceland is Icelandic, we may perhaps add that the relation of Caesar's Latin to the modern languages of Italy, Portugal and Spain is about the same as the relation of modern Icelandic to the current languages of Denmark, Norway and Sweden. This is, of course, merely rewording what we have said in two or three other places, that modern Icelandic is practically the same as the language of the sagas. This morning's Reykjavik newspaper differs less from the *Heimskringla* as Snorri wrote it in the thirteenth century than a London newspaper differs from *Hamlet* as Shakespeare wrote it in the seventeenth.

The Icelandic money unit is the krona (plural kronur) which is divided into 100 aurar. At the bank 4.40 kronur equal one American dollar, but throughout this book we have, for simplification, assumed when small amounts were dealt with that the krona has roughly the value of an American quarter or a British shilling—with large figures we have translated kronur into dollars at the 4.40 rate. The purchasing power of the krona within the country is about double that of the quarter in America or the shilling in Britain.

Most of the steamers discharge passengers at Reykjavik, the seat of government and of the larger cultural institutions. Foreign visitors are apt to call it a "quaint town." Icelanders do not object, or will not if in your vocabulary quaint implies youth, for Reykjavik is so young a city that one might say it has just been born—it has 40,000 people now but had 8000 only thirty years ago. It is situated on Faxa Bay, on the southwest coast, and has an excellent harbor. As we said in the first chapter: Ingolf considered that the choice was made by the gods, and many feel the gods chose well.

There are good hotels in Reykjavik, of which the most modern is the Borg, partly state-owned. Its rates (European plan) range from $1.75 to $4.00, depending on the accommodation desired (single or double room, with or without bath). Luncheon costs around $1.00 and dinner $1.00 to $1.50. It is the only hotel in the country licensed to serve wines and liquors. There is dancing in the evening.

Hotel Island (i.e., Iceland) is also excellent. Rates are from $1.00 to $3.00; luncheon is 75¢ and dinner 75¢ to $1.25. A flat rate on meals per day is offered at $2.80 to $4.00. Like the Borg, it has dancing in the evening.

The Gardur is a students' hostel which is used as a hotel in summer. Foreign visitors like to stay at Gardur. It is well run. Its rate of $2.50 per day includes both room and meals.

Other small, well-run and extremely moderate hotels are the Vik, Skjaldbreid and Hekla.

July and August are the best months for traveling, although June and September may be fairly well relied upon. From late in May until the beginning of August there is perpetual daylight; one can read a book the whole night through. On the longest day the sun does not set until 11:00 P.M. in the southern part of Iceland; at some points in the north the midnight sun is visible for about two weeks.

If you plan to take your trips in automobiles only there is no need for any special kind of clothing. On horseback tours you will need ordinary warm, strong traveling clothes; and you should take oilskins, a sou'-wester and waterproof riding boots.

Ponies can be hired for about $1.00 a day each, and a

guide is available at about the same price. The number of ponies needed depends on the sort of trip and the amount of baggage. For trips of a day or longer each rider wants two ponies, one to relieve the other after a certain number of hours. Whether it is cheaper to buy ponies or rent them depends upon the time you plan to spend in the country. If you have only a few days renting is better. If your visit lasts weeks, then you will economize through buying the number of ponies needed and selling them just before your departure. You will not get back what you paid for them, but you will save as compared with what would have been the rental fees.

Many of the trips which we outline call for pony rides, so we repeat what we have said about ponies earlier, that they are small, strong and gentle. Lord Dufferin said of his mount that it was "sure-footed enough to walk downstairs backwards." They are endearing creatures. Mistreatment of them is rare, for even the tourist usually develops a personal relation to his horse, be the association one of a few days only.

It is practically impossible to give an adequate brief description of the countryside. Wherever you go there are peculiarities, charms and surprises. The whole central section is mountainous. There are frequent mountain glaciers but, generally speaking, the land slopes down into great fertile plains or deep narrow valleys where the soft lines of green hills and winding clear rivers are broken by rugged lava. In some places steam rises out of the earth where the hot springs and geysers are boiling underneath. Most of the big rivers are now spanned with bridges so it is only in imagination that we feel the stress of the olden days when a crossing meant that both man and pony had to muster all strength and courage. The rivers themselves, usually of a powerful current, sometimes flow peacefully, while sometimes they plunge thunderously from great heights, adding beauty and variety of sight and sound to your journey.

The volcanic eruptions which largely created Iceland have left their signs everywhere, not only in the mountains but also in the great plains so covered with lava that they appear as if a furious sea had been turned to stone. During recent years volcanic eruptions have not been frequent, and mostly they have taken place in the interior, away from human habitation.

When you come to Iceland you will do best if you turn to Statourist. The service is free, and they will advise you judiciously on what to see in the time and with the money at your disposal. If you have special interests, such as mountain climbing or salmon fishing, trips can be planned with those in mind.

The trips here described are only a few of those which may be taken during a stay of from three to fourteen days.

Reykjavik–Geysir–Thingvellir: This is a three-day trip by motorcar. You will cross Hellisheidi (Cavern Heath), a plateau of lava more or less overgrown with moss and primitive plants which, after thousands of years, are trying to turn the rock into fertile soil. On the edge of

Hellisheidi you will have a view of a wide plain surrounded by mountains. With fair visibility, you will see the beautiful Eyjafjallajökull (Island Mountain Glacier) sixty miles away. A little later Hekla comes into view. Once it was considered that this volcano proved the existence of hell—it could be nothing else but the chimney of the dark abode. The name found its way into the languages of other people, for from it come the "Get you to Heckenfjaeld!" of the Danes, the "To Hackleberg!" of the north Germans, and the "To John Hackleburne's house!" of the Scotch. You pass the river Sog and make a short stop at an extinct crater of a peculiar shape named Ker (The Caldron). Then you head for Geysir (the Gusher), a spurting caldron that has given its name to like springs throughout the world.

Because geyser of English and similar words of many other languages come from the proper name of this gusher, we must stop to say that in Icelandic the general name for such springs is *kver*. Only one of the numerous *kvers* of Iceland is called Geysir—the one we are now describing. Russell says of it:

The area dominated by the springs is directly at the foot of Laugarfell, indeed the south side of this mountain once formed a portion of the hot section. This portion of the mountain is . . . marked by ruined geyser mounds, smeared with sticky clay of many colors, punctured with tiny fumaroles whence issue wavering wands of steam, while in many places rivulets of hot water break through the pasty crust. The area of real activity is about 3000 feet by 1800 feet. . . . Cast a stick, a straw, or a bit of paper where the spray will fall on it and in a day it will have become petrified and cemented to the rock beneath.

Russell had to wait many hours before Geysir erupted. Then:

. . . Everyone rushed to the elevation across from *Geysir's* runway. Again the rumble, heavier than before. The water is agitated in the basin, it boils up suddenly, subsides, the earth beneath our feet trembles and a mass of steaming water rises in the center of the basin to an elevation of fifteen feet and overflows the rim with a noisy splash. . . . A few moments of quiet expectation followed. Then, without further warning, a column of superheated water, ten feet in diameter, shot like a rocket into the air to the height of one hundred and twenty-five feet and the abysmal forces maintained that column for ten minutes. . . . The roar of falling water filled the air to the exclusion of all voices and flowed in hissing cascades down the slope, into the ravine and across the meadow to the river. . . . Volume upon volume of steam . . . belched into the air expanding under the reduced pressure and filled the air to the shutting out of the sun. Fountains of foam well over the brink. Explosion follows explosion and still that lofty tower of boiling water stands erect and masses of water fall to earth with a terrific crash. The column wavers, totters, falls. The eruption is over . . . and we rush up the dripping slope of geyserite, step over the rim into the hot basin and peer down into these depths whence came those rivers of water. . . .

If you reach Geysir in one of its quiet moods it is a good idea to stay overnight so as not to miss seeing it perform. But if you are lucky and are shortly presented with a scene such as Russell describes, you might forthwith proceed to Gullfoss, the golden waterfalls. This huge, thundering cataract sparkles in all colors when the sun strikes the spray. Russell says of it:

We turned to the north where the thunders of the falls boomed from beyond the cliffs and the mists glistened high in the air. No falls, not even the river is visible, they are embedded in the canyon a mile beyond. The crashing roar of the water increased and turning an angle of the cliffs the steeds paused upon the brink of the *Hvita* canyon. The full glory of the falls burst upon us radiant in its sheaf of rainbows. Leaving the ponies to graze upon the brink, we descended the crumbling wall to the level of the triangular area within the canyon. This grassy mist-washed mass of rock is on a level with the top of the lower falls, the real plunge of the *Hvita* into the lava abyss. As far as the mass of water is concerned this fall is the largest, not only in Iceland but in all Europe.

He calls the Gullfoss "grim, grand and glorious" but considers its setting even more impressive.

Above the plain *Lang Jökull* stretches forty miles across the horizon, lifting its unexplored surface of adamantine ice high in air, a perpetual challenge to him who would search the unknown. At its base and near at hand *Hvitavatn*, White-River-Lake . . . carries a fleet of icebergs on its sunlit surface. In the perpetual sunlight of Iceland's summer months this vast icefield discharges constant floods down its cliffs. Hence the *Hvita* starts upon its turbulent course to the sea. . . . Towards the east the peaks of

Kerlingafjall, Old-Women-Peaks, arrest the eye, around whose skirts hot springs are scattered sending up a mass of vapor like incense to the heroic gods of Scandinavian mythology.

Having seen Gullfoss, you would proceed to Laugarvatn, one of the country schools that are used as summer hotels. The building is heated with water from the springs on the edge of the lake, and there is a warmed indoor swimming pool.

If you have not stayed overnight at the Geysir you may stay here at Laugarvatn or proceed on to a pleasant inn called Thrastalundur, on the river Sog. Leaving this, you go up along the river and cross it over a bridge close by the large hydroelectric station which has recently been opened to increase the power supply for Reykjavik. From that point you would drive along the shore of the beautiful Thingvalla Lake to Thingvellir. Thingvellir (the Plain of Assembly or Parliament) has been closely linked to the whole national life for centuries. But there is more than historical interest, as Howell tells us:

After crossing the lava plain . . . the track leads up the steep ascent to Mosfellsheithi. A height of about one thousand feet is soon attained, and an undulating plateau lies before us. The trend is downwards, and soon the wilderness of wild chaotic rockland gives way to grassy grave-like hummocks. . . . Presently, through gorges on our right, the placid waters of Thingvallavatn, the second largest lake in Iceland, come in sight, with the black crater mouths of Sandey and Nesey peering up as islands. In an hour . . . the traveller finds himself upon the verge of the world-renowned Almannagja, or All-Men's-rift, a chasm 180 feet in depth. Before him lies a mighty lava stream that was old a thousand years ago. . . .

. . . Let us descend . . . to the grassy moat-like bottom of the rift. Half a mile beyond, the Öxara leaps down the rock wall in a clear transparent waterfall; and dashes on among the boulders which have been piled up within the rift. Here the inner wall has been disrupted, and the river foams among the debris, until it plunges into a dark, still pool. . . . Fording the river, we find ourselves upon the plain itself. It is mostly overspread with a cushion of soft, grey moss while little shrubberies of . . . birch, or willow bushes, rising sometimes to three or four feet high, are dotted up and down—where in unfrequented corners plover, ptarmigan and curlew may be found.

After having stayed the night at Thingvellir, you go on the third day towards Reykjavik, stopping on the way at Reykir to see how the natural heat is being used there to grow vegetables, fruit and flowers.

Reykjavik–Thjorsardalur–Hekla: An excellent idea is to combine the trip described above with an excursion to Hekla and to Thjorsardalur (the valley of the Thjorsa). Hekla is an easy climb and two hours will bring you to the top of it. Russell describes what you will see:

The view from Hekla is superb. The eye is first arrested by the ridges of lava, black, red, gray, horrent and ill-boding which extend down the mountain slopes. . . . Each of the two main ridges bisects a well-watered section, once fertile and now choked with sand. To the northwest, *Lang Jökull* raises its two score miles of ice parapet . . . to the northeast is spread out the vast expanse of mighty *Vatna Jökull* . . . an area of ice-covered tableland one hundred miles by sixty; between these two glaciers and directly north of us stands *Hofs Jökull*, Hof signifying heathen-temple. . . . Between the last two *Jökulls*, stretching away into the northeast, is the Sprengisander, Bursting-Sands, a mighty desert entirely void of vegetation. . . . Nearer, in the emerald plain flow the glacier-born rivers, the Thjorsa and the Hvita and a cloud of saffron sand floats in the air above the desert which we crossed yesterday. . . . Turn now to the southward, look down along the tumbled chimneys and the red hornitos of Hekla and the first object to arrest the eye is the beautiful Tindfjallajökull, Peaked-Ice Mountain [should be Peaked-Mountain-Glacier] with its two ice-horns . . . protruding from an oval mound of lava and casting their blue shadows on the trackless snow. Behind this mountain is the Saga country of the South, the home of the noble Njal and the peerless Gunnar. . . . Those ribbons of limpid silver that branch from the base of *Godalands Jökull*, Land-of-the-Gods, like reins from the hands of a chariot driver, those are the many branches of the Markarfjlot . . . pouring down its floods of glacial waters and volcanic sands. . . . Across the moors, the sheep ranges and the marshes beyond, the North Atlantic encircling the black masses of the Westman Islands, wreathes those weathered pillars with garlands of snow-white foam.

As mentioned before, it is easy to climb Hekla, but part of the way into the valley of Thjorsa you will ride a pony. The whole trip—Geysir, Gullfoss, Hekla, Thjorsardalur and Thingvellir—takes four or five days.

Thingvellir—the District of Borgarfjördur: Once you start riding the ponies you are apt to begin looking down upon automobile travel. Here is a suggestion:

You go by car to Thingvellir. Thence the ponies and a guide will take you right through the mountains along the Kaldidalur (The Cold Valley). As the name indicates, you will be traveling through a desolate place, a desert because it is solid rock, with huge glaciers on each side. At the same time you will be right in the middle of the majestic, clean and clear interior of the country, an experience not easily to be forgotten.

The first day's ride will end at a pleasant farmstead far up in the mountains on the side of the Borgarfjördur district. It will have been a rather strenuous day and you will be glad to take it more easily tomorrow. Then you will cross the Hvita (The White River), on horseback in order to reach the cave named Surtshellir. This subterranean passage is about one mile long, twelve yards wide and about ten yards high. It is dark inside; you should buy a flashlight or some candles before leaving Reykjavik. The part of the cave which usually stirs most interest is the Icicle Cave, the floor of which is of solid ice. Out of it stalagmites project, as stalactites do from the walls and ceiling, and your lights will create a child's dream of fairyland.

Icelandic folklore has many tales of Surtshellir. The best known concerns eighteen students from a divinity school who went to live there as outlaws with girls who eloped with them.

This trip would take four to five days, including a two-day stay at Reykholt, another of the charming natural-heated country schools, from which you will make shorter excursions.

A Ten to Twelve Day Trip: If you plan a longer journey you might combine the excursions through the south part of the country with one to Akureyri on the north coast, going from there to Myvatn and the interesting district which surrounds it. Myvatn means Mosquito Lake, and there you may find (almost) the only mosquitoes in the country—for Iceland differs pleasantly from most northerly districts, arctic and subarctic, in having practically no insect pests. This is no doubt because the drainage is so good in most places that they have no water to breed in.

The road from Reykjavik to the northland goes through the district of Borgarfjördur, saga country, where every farm is linked up with the traditions of a thousand years. The places of interest, both through beauty and history, are too many to name. Many travel books devote whole chapters to them and then apologize for skimping their subject.

The south and the north of Iceland are separated by a high plateau, the Holtavörduheidi, from which there are magnificent vistas, particularly because you can see much farther and more clearly in the dustless air of the North than in perhaps any country you have visited—unless you have been in the Arctic or Antarctic. Coming down from the plateau, you travel through the district of Hunavatnssysla with its lovely valleys up to Skagafjördur, which is not only beautiful but is also impressive; then the island of Drangey, associated with the tragedy of Grettir the Outlaw; the fertile plain through which the river Hjeradsvötn winds, and the stately mountains which shelter the district and from which it is easy to believe that the genii of ancient belief are still protecting the country.

Akureyri is the town next after Reykjavik in size, about 10,000. It is often called Iceland's northern capital. By its situation it is naturally a center for the northerly districts. Eyjafjördur (The Firth of Isles), on the west shore of which stands the city, cuts into just about the middle of the north coast and reaches far into the country. As it stretches farther inland it becomes gradually narrower; the last part is nearly cut in two by a sandbank reaching out from the west side. The narrow channel between the sandbank and the east coast of the firth leads into the fine harbor of Akureyri. A considerable part of the town is built on the sandbank (Oddeyri) and the whole town stretches from the point along the coast to the end of the harbor.

In spite of brisk activity Akureyri has an air of peace and serenity. The water of the harbor is usually quiet; the sheltering mountains appear to watch over the town. In summer everything is green and growing; for the soil is fertile and there are no harsh winds. The town is a cultural center, for it has, in addition to elementary schools, institutions of higher learning—preparatory, technical, domestic science and an agricultural experiment station.

A few miles inland from Akureyri is a sanatorium at Kristnes where Helgi the Lean, first settler of the district, raised his homestead a thousand years ago. The sanatorium has hot water heat which comes from the earth close by. For natural advantages Kristnes bears comparison with any mountain "cure" in the world. It stands on a ridge which flanks the whole valley; behind are the mountains; in front is the wide main valley and the winding river, Eyjafjardara.

The road leading from Akureyri to Myvatn crosses the Eyjafjardara where it spreads to form a delta before reaching the sea. This delta, like the whole valley, is specially fertile. Many birds nest in the small isles.

Immediately after crossing the delta, you would drive up the mountain Vadlaheidi. Russell says that:

The ascent of Vadlaheidi, Wade-Heath, in sunshine is one of the best rides in Iceland. The long fiord opens out to the Arctic Ocean at our feet and the distant *Jökulls* rise into prominence with diadems of ice upon their brows. The pastures on the lower slopes stud the valley with gems of emerald. Nearing the summit, we came upon the unmelted snows of winter, which were crusted sufficiently to support the horses. . . . At an elevation of 2300 feet above the fiord we reached a flat moorland which slopes gently, at first, toward the east. We paused . . . and stretched our-

Akureyri—"Capital of the North."

selves at length on a mound of Arctic flowers and gazed across the valley to the *Vindheima Jökull,* Home of the Winds.

Russell traveled by pony, but you may prefer a car. You will see more than glaciers—farmsteads and small villages scattered along the coast. There is much activity, for during the summer hundreds of motorboats and trawlers are bringing in their catches of herring. When you are atop Vadlaheidi at midnight in midsummer you can see a little slice of the sun just over the horizon —sky, sea and mountains fantastically decked in seemingly more colors than rainbows have.

To the south lies the valley of Eyjafjördur. Nearest is the river flowing through the lowland; then, in the distance, are the clear-cut mountains. You will proceed down the east side to the valley of the river Fnjoska where the remnants of a birch wood are only partly visible from the road. You will stop and stroll for a bit. The highest trees of this "forest" are thirty feet.

Crossing the bridge over the river, you will observe a change of vegetation. Low birch-bush and willow are everywhere. In spring and early summer they fill the air with fragrance.

Before long you will reach the Godafoss (Waterfall of the Gods) in the river Skalfandi (The Trembling River). Tradition says that the name of the falls is derived from a historical occasion when Thorgeir, a nobleman who was particularly instrumental in making Christianity the authorized religion in 1000, threw the images of his household gods into the falls. Again we borrow Russell's description:

An hour's ride . . . across the ancient lava bed brings the traveller to the bridge across the Skjalfandafljot, Trembling-River, and to the Godafoss . . . one of the most beautiful waterfalls in Iceland. It has not the grandeur of the Gullfoss . . . but its symmetrical formation and the two even sheets of water that pour over its brink unbroken make it very attractive. . . . The rocky islet (in the middle) is split asunder and a solid stream of water pours through the cleft forming a central fall. The spray and mist from the falls are visible for many miles around and to one accustomed to look for hot springs, whenever mists are seen rising in a column from the plain, this waterfall comes as a great surprise when one approaches the unexpected canyon.

You will stop for refreshment at Laugar (Warm Springs). Its springs were the principal reason for selecting it as a school site. In a coalless country it means a great deal to get an almost unlimited amount of scalding hot water free for heating, washing and swimming. Most of the country schools are erected at such places.

The district surrounding Myvatn has been described as "congealed pandemonium." Signs of volcanic convulsion are everywhere. You approach Myvatn at Skutustadir, a parsonage where the hospitable minister will put you up overnight. This place is on the southwest side of the lake, between extinct volcanoes.

Myvatn is the third largest lake in Iceland. Most of it is shallow—from three to twenty feet deep. It is almost entirely surrounded by lava, and lava flows have spread into it forming peninsulas and promontories. There are indentations without number; many of its islets are extinct volcanoes. A peninsula, Neslandatangi, runs out from the west coast and almost meets another from the east side, Landteigar. The lowland around the lake is only partly covered with grass, and the rest of it is lava. The surrounding mountains are impressive. You will notice here and there spots upon which it seems the sun is constantly shining. These are sulphur patches. In the seventeenth and eighteenth century quantities of sulphur were dug for export to Europe.

Of all the peculiar spots of the region you will want to see Dimmuborgir (The Dark Castles). This is a wild lava field where rise solitary volcanic castles, pillars and arches.

It is impossible to give an adequate description of all the strange, sometimes threatening, sometimes exquisite, places in this district. Russell has perhaps come nearest to it of those who write English:

The *Myvatn* region is the most fascinating, the most weird as well as the most beautiful place in all Iceland. I believe it to be the fairest spot in all that land of sun-kissed and wind-swept enchantment. The lake is twenty miles long and its deepest place is not over twelve feet. There are places where the water is hot and others where the water flows from under the lava in ice-cold streams into the lake. At the entrance of these streams there is excellent trout fishing. The lake is dotted with islands, each a small crater, each fringed to the edge of the water with the fragrant *Angelica*, each clothed with grass nearly to the summit and each summit black and red, scorched, blistered and horrent. Hundreds of these low craters fringe the southern end of the lake and are scattered over the adjoining farms. . . . They are an exact representation of the mountains of the moon as viewed through a powerful telescope. To the geologist the *Myvatn* craters are of rare interest, for nowhere else on the earth are they duplicated in the numbers and in their peculiar formation.

The road we have been following ends at the most impressive falls in the whole country, the Dettifoss of the river Jökulsa. This monarch of Icelandic falls is in one of the mightiest rivers of the country, Jökulsa a Fjöllum (Glacier River of the Mountains), whose waters plunge over a brink into a deep chasm with a force of half a million horsepower. Howell says of it:

The river runs through a fine gorge, two hundred and fifty feet in depth, and about as far beyond the gorge a rising cloud of curling mist-wreaths proclaims the presence of the waterfall. Passing at first a basalt ledge, the flood breaks up into rapids and dashes on to a spot where a rift in the lava has split its bed into a vast ravine, one hundred and eighty feet in perpendicular depth and five hundred feet across. Into this V-shaped cleft the already milk-white river hurls itself with a deafening roar in a sheet four hundred yards in width. Midway some knobs of basalt project and the wild rebound of the falling mass flings sheets of shattered foam into the awful sweep of the plunging flood, till the whole resembles a lambs' wool fleece depending from the crag. And this is set in the jaws of the black abyss, where nothing detracts from the startling but truly Icelandic contrast. Yet, however fine in its summer guise, it must surpass itself when in springtime, with a greater width by far, the mad career of huge blocks of ice hustling each other over the brink must form an almost appallingly grand scene, a continuous avalanche and waterfall combined.

Before returning to Reykjavik you might visit Asbyrgi, fifteen miles north of Dettifoss. This is a plateau sheltered by an encircling wall of perpendicular rock rising upwards from 120 to 270 feet. In the middle is a large perpendicular rock or island shaped like a horse's hoof. Therefore legend has it that the island is the hoofmark of Sleipnir, the steed of the god Odin.

It has been difficult to select routes to suggest. We must leave out so many which are as interesting and unusual. The east, for one thing, differs strikingly from the west. In the east we have, besides the long narrow fjords with steep mountains on both sides, such districts as the Fljotsdalshjerad with the great river Lagarfjlot. On the west coast, the more open districts around Breidifjördur (Broad Bay) are rich and picturesque. We have not even mentioned Snaefellsnes (the Peninsula of Snaefell) or Snaefellsjökull. In the southeast are some of the wildest of the inhabited districts in Iceland. Glaciers, comparatively near the coast, pour out freshets of water.

One of the small glacier rivers, the Skeidará, turns for a short period "every eight years" into a giant stream

several miles wide. The length of the interval between
floods and their approximately regular appearance
makes this one of Iceland's most tantalizing mysteries.
Many believe the floods are due to volcanic melting of
the lower side of the glacier. A theory has been advanced that a valley beneath the glacier, or some reservoir, is gradually filled with water produced by a volcanic heat that is fairly steady. The rate of melting would
be such that every eight years the valley or reservoir
would be filled and would begin overflowing. Then it
would be emptied, either by a siphon action (which seems
hard to believe) or more likely because the water starts
flowing over the ice dam and by stream erosion cuts it
down until the reservoir is emptied. Thereupon, you
would have to suppose by this theory, a new dam
would be formed and there would begin a new accumula-
tion of volcanically created thaw water.

Having digressed to explain the peculiarities of the
river Skeidará, we might perhaps digress further (and late
in our book!) to explain reference in several of our
chapters, and particularly in this one, to Icelandic rivers
as being large. This may seem strange for an island country no bigger than to be intermediate in size between
Ireland and Pennsylvania.

Naturally Iceland does not equal the United States in
the length or volume of its rivers; nor can she maintain
(even when Niagara has been excluded as being not,
strictly speaking, within the United States) that her
waterfalls are greater. Neither can Iceland match the

continent of Europe in the length or volume of the biggest river; but Iceland does claim waterfalls greater than any in Europe, measured in the horsepower which they might generate.

Horsepower is a product of declivity and volume. Grades in Iceland are steep because the mountains are high and the distance to the coast relatively short. The otherwise incredible volumes that pour through the rivers into the sea are due to the height of the mountains and the warmth of the Gulf Stream.

There are parts of the Icelandic lowland where rainfall is not heavy, not quite enough to please the farmers. But that is, at least partly, because mountains have captured water from the clouds. The humid Gulf Stream winds may not form clouds at sea, or when they pass the shoreline, but they do form them against the mountain slopes and peaks. Thus it comes about that mountains that are not a third as high as those of Switzerland and the United States have gathered in a country which is never as cold in winter as the mountainous districts of Switzerland and of the United States, glaciers that are far bigger than the largest of Switzerland or of the state of Washington, where the biggest American glaciers lie.

It is only in British Columbia and in Alaska that continental North America can match Iceland in glaciers, and then for the same reason. Just as the largest Icelandic glaciers are on her south coast so are the large glaciers of Alaska exclusively on her south coast. They are built up there against the mountains by winds from the Japan

Current just as Iceland's are built by those from the Gulf Stream.

We have said elsewhere that few months in Iceland will average below freezing—only January does at Reykjavik. There are thaws in every month in most of the country and in most months in every part of the country. This means that the peaks are not mere gatherers of snow, even in winter. They also turn their snow, or at least the snow of their slopes, into water that pours into the rivers. Thus you have the glaciers acting not merely as feeders of the streams but also as stabilizers of the flow, seeing to it through winter thaws that the horse-power of the waterfalls does not vary as much from season to season as does water power in most other parts of the world. Next to lakes such as those that feed Niagara, glaciers like those of Iceland are the best known stabilizers of river volume.

Nothing has been said about Iceland for winter sports, yet it is sure to become one of the popular choices of ski enthusiasts. The people, to whom skiing was formerly just a way of travel, have within the last two years taken it up as a sport and have brought to their clubs foreign instructors. True enough, the snowfields nearest Reykjavik (reached by automobile in a few hours) are not the finest in the country; but the operation of an air service throughout the winter will do away with the handicap of closed roads which once barred the south coast during winter from the excellent ski runs of the north.

Salmon and trout fishing bring many tourists to Iceland in the summer.

We close with an autumn word picture of scenery from the American, W. S. C. Russell, who, with Mrs Russell, came as a tourist:

The descending clouds and the falling snow suddenly shut off the view, but the camera of the eye has caught it all in a circling panorama and the prints are stored in memory's folder to be opened at leisure. The infinite waste of the lava billows, grandeur rising from desolation, the flash of the restless rivers, the quiet of the happy plain—these are but the halftones in Iceland's matchless print.

CHAPTER XIV

Icelanders in the Americas

IN 1851 two Icelandic Mormons from Copenhagen came as missionaries to the Westman Islands, southwestern Iceland. They succeeded in converting a few people. One of these became the first Icelandic emigrant to America.

In 1855 Thordur Thidriksson started out by way of Denmark and England for the Mormon settlements in Utah. The voyage across the Atlantic took seven weeks. Fifty people died, but Thidriksson reached New York on March 7, 1856, and made his way thence overland. Icelandic colonists followed him and a small settlement was founded at Spanish Fork, Utah. There were also a few Icelanders who remained in Salt Lake City. These settlements were never large.

Meantime Iceland was waging a seemingly hopeless struggle for political liberty. True enough, the Danish monopoly had been brought to an end in 1854; but the people were pressing on for more rights of self-government. This struggle developed with the years.

When success still appeared remote the people's newspapers (as distinguished from the government organ) began to suggest emigration as an escape from tyranny.

The Civil War in the United States may have been the chief reason why the first exodus was to South America. A popular view is that the Icelandic passion for coffee—great then and great still—was what really drew them—the thought that in Brazil they could grow their own.

One Icelander, Kristjan Gudmundsson, reached Brazil on March 30, 1863. He was followed six months later by four others, Jonas Einarsson and his son Jon, Jonas Hallgrimsson and Jonas Fridfinnsson, who were to pick out a site for an Icelandic colony. They were joined by others still later, some of whom traveled by way of Copenhagen and Hamburg where they attached themselves to German immigrant parties. The last Icelanders who went to Brazil as colonists started in 1873.

The descendants of some of these people still live in South America, but no true Icelandic colony was ever founded there. Several eventually moved to the United States or Canada. Others scattered through Brazil, moved to Chile and elsewhere.

In less than seven years after the first colonists had set out for Brazil, the things which the Icelanders valued most highly were being offered to all comers on the North American mainland. The Civil War in the United States was over; Alaska had been purchased. In the eastern states there was a feverish desire to colonize and develop the West. Railroads were being built and emigrants were flooding across the country. In Canada the political war was over and the Dominion had emerged triumphantly as a federated union. There the pioneer spirit developed, as it did across the border, except that a campaign to develop their West had to wait for the late seventies and early eighties.

But in Iceland advocates of liberty were being fined, jailed or exiled; freedom was checkmated everywhere, except in the hearts of the people. Economic and social conditions were wretched. It was still the custom for visitors to Iceland to have in the books which they afterwards published startling (and "smart") contrasts between the Danish and "native" homes.

In those days wages were high nowhere, of course, if figured in dollars. Rogers points out one fact which indicates why the homes of the Icelanders were poor and overcrowded. By Dane-imposed law, boys and girls over sixteen were compelled to work for wages. A girl was paid eight dollars a year. In Canada the same girl would be paid $205 a year.

Immigration to the United States was renewed in 1870 when four young Icelanders founded a settlement on Washington Island, Wisconsin. They were Jon Gislason, Arni Gudmundsson, Jon Einarsson and Gudmundur Gudmundsson. They were later joined by others. Some of their descendants still live at this settlement.

In 1872 a party of almost 300 Icelanders came to America. Among these the leaders were Sigtryggur Jonasson, one of the founders of New Iceland, Manitoba;

Pall Thorlaksson who founded the settlements in North Dakota and Hans Thorgrimsen who took the lead in forming the Icelandic Lutheran synod in America.

Jonasson sent to Iceland such glowing reports of Ontario that the next year 153 people left Akureyri, and thirty others soon followed. Their idea had been to settle in one place; but on reaching Canada some fifty of them decided to go to Wisconsin with Pall Thorlaksson, who had come out to join his parents. Others went to Nova Scotia. The majority settled in Muskoka, Ontario. Many who later became prominent among Icelanders in America were in this group, among them Stephan G. Stephansson, Baldwin L. Baldwinsson and Jon Jonsson Bardal. Jon Bjarnasson, eventually a leader in the Icelandic Lutheran church in America, also came that same year, on the recommendation of his friend Pall Thorlaksson.

In this period of taking root anew Icelandic culture was not neglected. In 1874 an Icelandic Society, *Islendingafélag*, was formed to foster intellectual pursuits. The desire for a united colony, in which such interests could better be pursued, grew more and more strong. When Wisconsin failed to provide the desired opportunity various committees were formed to look elsewhere. Sigfus Magnusson and Jon Halldorsson went to Nebraska. On the strength of their report a few Icelanders eventually settled there.

During the struggle against the Danes which was at its height in the early seventies a student named Jon Olafsson had to flee Iceland because of what the Danish power considered treasonable utterances. He first escaped to Europe and then made his way to the United States. Poet, adventurer, and in his early days distinctly of the type said to live by their wits, Olafsson had not been long in the United States when he discovered a situation he thought he could capitalize.

Grant was having many troubles with the presidency. One of them was Alaska which, through being Seward's Icebox and Seward's Folly, was to the Democrats a folly of the Republican party and therefore President Grant's folly, he being a Republican. Olafsson's bright idea was to go to the President, relying on what was sure to be the President's idea—that Iceland was a land of ice and snow such as Alaska was also at that time supposed to be.

Blond, handsome, well over six feet, in command of several modern languages and versed in Greek and Latin, this young man claimed to demonstrate in his own person to the President that while Icelanders were as hardy as the Eskimos are supposed to be they were nevertheless a white people, a desirable type of European—in short, a godsend to the harassed administration, one of whose unsolved difficulties had been proving to the country that Alaska was neither Seward's nor anybody else's folly.

The President took the bait. Jon Olafsson and two compatriots, Olafur Olafsson and Pall Björnsson, were commissioned to visit Alaska so that they might return to Iceland and report that here were a country and a people mutually adapted.

As he told of it afterwards, the Alaska journey was to Olafsson at the time not much more than a student prank. However, the report he made shows at least a bit of discrimination, mixed with the tongue-in-cheek features. For he differentiates between localities as suited or not suited to settlement from Iceland. He recommends specially Kodiak Island and its vicinity, of which he says: "We cannot, therefore, do otherwise than express the hope that the American Government will do all that lies in its power to encourage the immigration of our countrymen to Alaska, as the land seems to have been created just for them. In like manner we think that men of our race are the best adapted to settle and cultivate that country, and to utilize the natural resources."

The report, which was also signed by Olaf Olafsson and Pall Björnsson, concludes with the statement they are convinced that Alaska will suit their countrymen "better than any other land on earth."

The government evidently thought that the report would be useful in bringing Icelanders to the Territory, for they authorized its publication in the Icelandic language, *Alaska, Lysing a landi og landskostum*, etc., Washington, 1875. This may have been the first Icelandic language publication to appear in the United States. It is forty-eight pages long. A six-page English language abstract was published, Washington, 1875.

It is not on record that when Olafsson returned to Iceland a few years later he was a propagandist for Alaska. Nor have we found any record of a con-

siderable number of Icelanders going there till the Yukon
and the Alaska gold rushes of around 1900.

A light is thrown upon the mental processes of this
adventurer by a sonnet which has been translated by
Professor Kirkconnell:

ALASKA

I rest in cooling shadows of the pines
On softest grasses by the ocean-shore;
The heart finds solace from its sad designs
In bird-song and the sea-waves muffled roar.
It seems to me I know this cliff of old,
It seems to me my exile is forgot,
It seems to me a wanderer could behold
A welcome home on this majestic spot.

But near at hand debauchery most foul
Breaks in upon the beauty of the wild
And mars the quiet of the wilderness—
Not here, Alaska, where the sin-hounds howl,
Will any exiled, lorn Icelandic child
Find home and fosterland for his distress.

What vice Olafsson discovered in Alaska is anybody's
guess. It may have been rum sales to the natives. It may
quite as well have been the activities of the Russian
Orthodox Church. For to the devout Lutheran of that
time a movement towards a Catholic church, whether
English, Roman or Greek, would have appeared a but
slightly circuitous approach to the gates of hell.

In Executive Document No. 48, Senate, First Session,
Forty-fourth Congress, we have a letter from the secre-

tary of war transmitting information from Captain J. W. White, showing that in 1876 Jon Olafsson's ideas were in favor—including some of those on moral elevation:

Do you not think that it would be good country for the Icelanders who are leaving their country; and they not be our best means of developing the resources of Alaska, and of rightly dealing with and elevating both the Aleuts and the Kolosh Indians? Yes; the very best defense we could have, and the best colonists to save the country and the people. The sober, industrious Icelanders would soon make a Territory and ultimately a State, of great value to our American Union. To move ten or twenty thousand of them there, would be the grandest enterprise of the nation, and grant them lands and a home free.

Brigadier General O. O. Howard, commanding the Department of Columbia (under which came Alaska) wrote from Portland, Oregon, March 2, 1876, with regard to Alaska colonization by Icelanders, that "Undoubtedly, every possible facility should be given to the colonists who come well prepared to develop the resources of that country, and who would soon afford us a steady and reliable basis for a territorial government."

Meantime, the Canadian government had interested itself in colonization to the extent of sending paid agents to Iceland to divert the tide of emigrants to the Dominion. Lord Dufferin, then governor general, had been in Iceland in 1856 and had written that

The Icelanders are . . . by all accounts, the most devout, innocent, pure-hearted people in the world. Crime, theft, debauchery, cruelty, are unknown among them; they have neither prison, gallows, soldiers nor police; and in the manner of the lives they lead . . . there is something of a patriarchal simplicity . . .

He was active in the colonizing movement.

In 1874 the St Patrick arrived in Quebec harbor with 365 Icelanders aboard. A government official, accompanied by Johannes Arngrimsson, met them and tried to persuade them to settle in Canada. The newcomers had intended to go to the United States where they believed they would have greater freedom. The Dominion thereupon offered them the right of citizenship at once, and a tract of land for a colony. They agreed to remain in Canada.

This group went first to Kinmount in the backwoods of Ontario, about sixty miles north of Toronto, where a railway was being built. Not long after their arrival the railway construction was suspended and the Icelanders, who had been able to bring with them only modest supplies of money and goods, were in grave difficulties. The land was poor and cultivation was disappointing.

In 1874 Johannes Arngrimsson, now a government immigration agent, offered the Kinmount settlers land in Nova Scotia. The spring of 1875 about eighty families moved there, and others followed them. They founded and settled Markland. Meantime, on the representations of Arngrimsson, colonists came to this settlement also direct from Iceland. For these settlers the Canadian government provided cabins and a certain amount of livestock. At one time Markland had some 200 people. Among them was Brynjolfur Brynjolfsson who worked tirelessly for their welfare. Later one of his sons became the first Icelandic member of a state legislature of the United States—in North Dakota.

But the soil was poor, stubbornly forested and with large boggy or stony patches, so within a year there began an exodus. By 1882 only one Icelander remained in the province, Sigaretha Thorsteine (doubtless Sigridur Thorsteinsdottir) who had left the colony for Chaswood and had there married a Canadian, Porter Taylor. Her descendants still live in Chaswood. One of her sons reports that the Icelandic settlement is now completely overgrown and that only three or four graves are left to tell that the people had ever been there.

The colonists had, as we have said, a good friend in Lord Dufferin. The Kinmount settlement had another in John Taylor. Dufferin persuaded the government to grant the Icelanders financial aid in moving their colony to a new site, and Taylor volunteered to help them select it. In 1875 a committee led by Sigtryggur Jonasson and guided by Taylor began their search for a suitable tract. They selected a strip of land along the west shore of Lake Winnipeg and named it New Iceland. The first settlement was called Gimli, from the Promised Land of the Eddaic religion.

Margaret McWilliams says of the settlement that

Delegates came out to view the land and with all the wheat-growing area to choose from, selected the inaccessible shore of Lake Winnipeg. One of their number has set out the reasons for their choice. The grasshoppers would not be so likely to do damage on the shores of the lake.[1] There was abundant timber for building and for fuel. There was a waterway to Winnipeg, and, likewise, an abundance of fine fish. Large tracts of land could be secured where the Icelanders might live by themselves. Lastly, the main line of the projected railway was going to cross the river at Selkirk, only forty miles away.

In October 1875 the settlers began to arrive. In the first party were eighty-five families (285 people). Again quoting Miss McWilliams:

The winter that year was long and severe, but these new settlers built themselves shelters and carried on the work of making a home and winning a livelihood in the wilderness. Despite the hardships, the reports which went back to Iceland brought out another party the following year.

By 1876 the colony had grown to some 1400 people and a council of five was appointed for temporary local government.

Meanwhile, in the United States, there began a movement into Minnesota. This was started by Gunnlaugur Petursson and his wife Gudbjorg Jonsdottir who moved to that state from Wisconsin. They were later followed by others. They did not form as Icelandic a settlement as Gimli, for people of other nationalities were also there, but Icelanders became numerous particularly around

[1] Editor's note: The prairie provinces and prairie states had suffered repeated grasshopper invasions in the preceding years which had devastated crops over large areas.

Minnesota and Marshall. By 1878 this group had organized a society for the purchasing of books and the holding of religious services. The first clergyman who visited them, and who helped with organization, was the Rev. Pall Thorlaksson. Four congregations were established, all of which were served by one minister.

The immigrants in this period took their Lutheranism seriously. There were affiliations with the German Lutheran Missouri synod and with the Norwegian Lutheran synod. There were other affiliations, and there were people without affiliation. Differences which seem slight to an outsider were burning issues, and communities were sharply divided. Like the effects of a mustard plaster, the irritation of these schisms may have tended to keep the immigrants from worrying about what you would think were more serious troubles, such as are described by Miss McWilliams:

The difficulties which this settlement encountered would have defeated a less sturdy people. Especially sad is the story of the smallpox plague which visited it in the fall of 1877. The colony was cut off for weeks from communication with the world outside and more than fifty persons died. The growth of industry brought to them employment, but under conditions which called for courage and hardihood. Bad roads frustrated many of their efforts and thirty long years lay between their coming and that of the first railroad to Winnipeg.

In 1877 there began the organization of a permanent local government for New Iceland. The colony was divided into four settlements, Vidinesbygd, Arnesbygd, Fljotsbygd and Mikleyjarbygd, each of which elected one man. The four together, with a president and vice-president, served as council. A constitution was framed in 1878. Gjerset says of it:

This fundamental law, the only one of its kind among the Icelanders in America, remained in force till 1887. New Iceland was a state with its own constitution, laws and government, even its own language and distinct nationality. No other people than the Icelanders were allowed to settle within its borders. But in all except local affairs it remained under the authority of the Canadian government.

Poverty and epidemics notwithstanding (at one period the Canadian government granted the colonists financial aid and Norwegians in the United States raised a relief fund for them), the New Icelanders forged ahead. In 1877 they organized the *Prentfélag Nyja Islands* (New Iceland Printing Company), to issue books and journals. On September 10 of that year the first Icelandic newspaper, *Framfari* (Progress), began to appear under the editorship of Halldor Briem. This paper, which ceased publication in 1880, is important as source material for the early history of the colony. Several other publications were started; they ran their course and ceased to be. Two Icelandic weekly newspapers are now current: *Heimskringla* and *Lögberg*, both of Winnipeg. New Iceland is still flourishing. It has sent to the Manitoba legislature several able men.

A combination of religious and economic difficulties

led to an emigration from New Iceland. In the spring of 1879 the Rev. Pall Thorlaksson and a committee began their search for new land. Thorlaksson went through part of Minnesota and through the southern part of Dakota Territory while Sigurdur Josua and Magnus Stefansson scouted around Pembina County in Dakota (now North Dakota) at the suggestion of the editor of the Winnipeg *Standard* who considered that all the best Minnesota land had already been taken up.

On this trip Josua and Stefansson took up land west of Cavalier. Returning to Pembina to file their claims, they met the rest of the party. Again they started out, this time going farther west and south near the foot of the Pembina Mountains, where now are the towns of Mountain and Gardar. Pall Thorlaksson took up land for himself and others at Mountain, Johann Hallson took up land to the northeast at the present Hallson. During the summer some ten people filed claims. In the three or four years following a real Icelandic migration began. Settlers came from New Iceland, Nova Scotia, Wisconsin, Minnesota, while some came direct from Iceland. Within ten years the Pembina colony was one of the largest in America.

In 1880 Thorlaksson founded the first congregation. On March 12, 1882, he died. Gjerset says of him: "Brave, gentle and resourceful, a true friend and a devoted leader, he had worn himself out in untiring effort to aid his people in their various needs."

The town of Pembina was the center of the Dakota

colony, though by 1882 all the land had been taken up and colonists were spreading out to Cavalier County, still farther west to Mouse River in Dakota, and to Rosseau County, Minnesota, about 100 miles east of the Pembina settlement. In 1884 the Rev. Hans Thorgrimsen, who had succeeded Thorlaksson as minister, proposed that all the Icelandic congregation should unite and form an Icelandic Lutheran synod. A meeting was held in Mountain, North Dakota, and a constitution written which was ratified at a later one in Winnipeg. It was signed by thirteen congregations.

Many Icelanders in the Pembina settlement have become prominent in affairs of their state, and Pembina County has repeatedly been represented by Icelanders in both houses of the state legislature.

While New Iceland was being settled many Icelanders came to Winnipeg. Some of them remained and founded a colony which dates from the New Iceland period. Since it was located in the chief point of communication for midwestern Canada, it attracted other Icelanders and eventually became the center of Icelandic intellectual life in America. By 1877 it had organized a society which guided immigrants, aided the needy and educated children. At first this was called *Islendingafélag*, but in 1881 the name was changed to *Framfarafélag*. Its purpose was broadened to include every activity that would be of benefit to the Icelanders and it continued active for nearly twenty-five years.

In 1884 the Rev. Jon Bjarnasson returned from Iceland

and organized the Winnipeg Icelanders into a congregation. The first church was built in 1887. Gjerset says of this pastor: "He was not only a learned man and an able speaker but an inspiring leader, more highly beloved and honored by his people than any other Icelander in America." At the time of his death in 1914 he was president of the Icelandic Lutheran synod. A small Unitarian synod was also established and many prominent Icelanders are in its congregation.

About 6000 Icelanders are now living in Winnipeg. Most of them are prosperous, and many are active in civic life.

From the parent settlement of New Iceland colonists spread throughout Canada and the United States. In August 1880 Sigurdur Kristofersson and Kristjan Jonsson took up land at Argyle, 100 miles southwest of Winnipeg, and in March of the following year other colonists followed them with ox sleds on which they had built little houses for their families. About four years later there were sixty farm homes in the settlement.

Thingvalla, 250 miles northwest of Winnipeg, was started by Helgi Jonsson in 1885. This is a small settlement and sparsely populated.

About 1886 Icelanders began to pioneer near Shoal Lake and Swan Lake, northwest of Winnipeg, on the east side of Lake Manitoba. A few years later several Icelandic settlements were started on the western shores of Lake Manitoba. The colonists spread out to Swan River, northwest of Winnipeg, Pine Valley (later Piney), southeast of Winnipeg, Laufas settlement, southwest of Winnipeg, and Brown, about nine miles south-west of Morden. There were also two settlements founded in Ontario, near the Manitoba border, at Lake Dauphin and Keewatin.

Icelandic settlements in Alberta began in 1888, the majority coming there from North Dakota. A few settled in Calgary but most of them took up homesteads near Red Deer and Markerville.

The Icelandic settlement in Saskatchewan is today the largest rural concentration of Icelanders in North America. An area ten miles from north to south and forty-eight miles from east to west is mainly populated by 4000 Icelanders. Wynyard is the center of this district. The settlement, some 400 miles northwest of Winnipeg, was founded in the summer of 1891 by two farmers from the Thingvalla colony, Ingimundur Eiriksson and Kristian Helgason. Five families joined them the same summer. From 1892 to 1909 there was a steady influx from various settlements.

Other colonists went to the Pacific coast and small settlements may be found in Vancouver and Victoria, British Columbia, on the Canadian side of the line; and at Blain, Point Roberts, Bellingham and Seattle in the state of Washington, with smaller groups in other coast cities.

By 1900 emigration from Iceland had practically ceased. Holme quotes Icelandic statistics to show that in the period 1870–1900 about 25,000 people emigrated to the Americas—or about one third of the entire population of Iceland. There are few countries that have sent a higher percentage to the United States and Canada. He estimates that in 1921 there were some 40,000 Icelanders and their descendants in the Americas, 30,000 of whom are in Canada. This is higher than the census figures which, however, are beyond doubt low through faulty classification. The Canadian official count for 1931 is 19,382.

In the United States the largest concentrations are still found in Minnesota and the Dakotas, but it is likely enough that there are some Icelanders now in every state of the Union.

The foregoing shows that while the Icelanders tended to form strictly national communities wherever they went, individuals and families did not always stay in any one community but moved into and out of province and state as if there were no international boundary. In that sense, what is said of one group or settlement may be considered as applying to all of them.

In 1877, two years after the founding of New Iceland, Lord Dufferin visited the settlement. He assured the people "in terms which made them proud indeed, that a more valuable accession to the intelligence, patriotism, loyalty, industry and strength of the country had never been introduced into the Dominion."

Miss McWilliams quotes with agreement W. D. Scott's appraisal of the colonists thirty years after their first arrival:

The difficulties in a man's way often bring out the best that is in him. Whether or not this was the reason of the success of the Icelanders, it is certain that their progress has been phenomenal. In a power to acquire a knowledge of the English language, they are in a class by themselves. An Icelander who knows no word of English when the ground is being prepared for seed in the spring will speak that language with scarcely a trace of foreign accent by the time the harvest is being garnered in the fall. . . . No people show a stronger desire for the education of their children. As a result, they are, considering their numbers, prominent in mercantile, professional and political life.

It is fortunate for the Icelanders that, although they reside in two countries of America, those two countries have an affectionate respect for each other. This has enabled the Icelandic citizens of the United States and those of Canada to maintain both the old loyalties and the new. Miss McWilliams has said of those in Canada: ". . . of all the peoples who have come to Manitoba, (they) have most quickly become identified with the British population and have made most progress in the general life of the province." To the extent that this is true for Canada it will be true also for the United States.

But in back of it all, and running through it all, is love for the mother country. The Federal Writers' volume on North Dakota says for that state:

An artistic and deeply imaginative people . . . they still retain many of their old Icelandic traditions and arts. . . . They take great pleasure in preserving their native culture.

ACKNOWLEDGMENT

APPENDIX A of this volume lists the main sources of each chapter; but it is well to emphasize that chief dependence has been upon material furnished by various departments of the Icelandic government through Iceland's Commissioner General to the New York World's Fair 1939, Mr Vilhjalmur Thor. The illustrations are from material furnished by Statourist, the official (government) tourist agency at Reykjavik. One of the two maps is used by courtesy of Earl Hanson and the American Geographical Society of New York; the other by courtesy of *Foreign Affairs*.

The bibliography shows many sources for the chapter "Icelanders in America," but special thanks for material are due to Mr Thorl. Thorfinnson, of Mountain, North Dakota, and to Professor Richard Beck of the University of North Dakota.

Members of the staffs of several universities have collaborated, among them Manitoba, North Dakota and Yale. Two universities were called upon for specially heavy contributions:

The Library of Cornell University, Ithaca, New York, has the largest Icelandic collection in America, founded and endowed by Willard Fiske. In charge is Professor Halldor Hermannsson, a world leader in Icelandic scholarship. Many questions have been referred to him and have been settled with a better chance of correctness than anyone else could have given. But he has ruled merely upon separate points, so that he does not bear responsibility for either trend of thought or manner of presentation.

Through Professor F. Stanton Cawley and Mr Thomas F. Currier, the Widener Library of Harvard University undertook to prepare a bibliography of works in English which deal with Iceland or with Icelandic subjects. The manuscript arrived in time, but it proved so bulky that using it would have doubled the size of our volume—or, rather, would have made necessary a work in two volumes. This bibliography, therefore, must await a later publication. Meantime readers who do not use easily a language other than English will have to content themselves with picking out the English language references from the magnificent bibliography, in two quarto volumes, published by Cornell University under the editorship of Professor Hermannsson, *Catalogue of the Icelandic Collection Bequeathed by Willard Fiske*, Ithaca, New York, 1914, and Ithaca and London, 1927.

As said, the basic material of this volume is published reports and written statements from various departments of the Icelandic government. Their chief merits are being up to date and reliable. Their chief defect is an Icelandic point of view, for the reader can grasp qualities and problems more easily when presented through foreign eyes—through travelers who have written on Iceland in various languages and through scholars who have made their studies without a pro-Iceland nationalist bias. To get the benefit of the obviously desirable outside judgment we have examined several hundred volumes on Iceland or Icelandic problems; chiefly works in English, for they serve better the reader of this book. Many of the facts and views of these foreigners cover the same ground as statements which had been furnished by the Icelandic government. In such cases we have substituted, by quotation or paraphrase, the presentation of the foreign writers.

In checking, sorting and assembling the Icelandic material and in comparing it with non-Icelandic publications, I have had the assistance of my research associates Mrs Olive R. Wilcox, Mrs Genevieve N. Shipman and Miss Olga Dalman. Most of the preliminary recasting was done by Mrs Shipman; much of the editorial checking as well as the proofreading was by Mrs Wilcox; some work under both divisions, as well as the typing, was by Miss Dalman.

The outstanding good fortune of this book is that Theodore Roosevelt, Jr, on reading the manuscript, experienced some revival of his youthful interest in the sagas as well as a kindling of new interest through learning how a country without any soil for standard agriculture, without gold, petroleum or other economic minerals, abjectly poor as late as 1854 when it secured its commercial independence, has through democratic process managed to come about as near as any democracy in the world to abolishing poverty, reaching at the same time many collateral goals. So, for reasons of the past and present, he came to a mood for introducing to their English-speaking fellow Americans that little-known nation which introduced the American mainland to Europe 939 years ago.

VILHJALMUR STEFANSSON

New York, N.Y.
May 29, 1939

APPENDIX A

BIBLIOGRAPHY

Iceland and Its History

Banks, Joseph.—*See* Troil, below.

Bryce, Viscount James, *Studies in History and Jurisprudence*, Vol. I, Oxford, 1901.

Dasent, George Webbe, "Introduction and Life of Richard Cleasby," in Gudbrand Vigfusson, *An Icelandic-English Dictionary*, Oxford, 1875.

Gjerset, Knut, *History of Iceland*, New York, 1924.

Hermannsson, Halldor, "Modern Icelandic," *Islandica*, Vol. XII, Ithaca, N.Y., 1919.

——— "Eggert Olafsson," *Islandica*, Vol. XVI, Ithaca, 1925.

——— "The Book of the Icelanders (*Íslendingabók*)" by Ari Thorgilsson, edited and translated with an Introductory Essay and Notes, *Islandica*, Vol. XX, Ithaca, 1930.

Hooker, William Jackson, *Journal of a Tour in Iceland in the Summer of 1809*, privately printed, Yarmouth, 1811.

Horrebow, N., *The Natural History of Iceland*, London, 1758.

Kirkconnell, Watson, *The North American Book of Icelandic Verse*, New York and Montreal, 1930.

Kneeland, Samuel, *An American in Iceland*, Boston, 1876.

Mackenzie, Sir George Steuart, *Travels in the Island of Iceland during the Year MDCCX*, 2nd edition, Edinburgh, 1812.

Olafsen & Povelsen, Messrs, *Travels in Iceland: Performed by Order of His Danish Majesty*, London, 1805.

Taylor, Bayard, *Egypt and Iceland in the Year 1874*, 1st edition, New York, 1874.

Thorsteinsson, Thorsteinn (editor), *Iceland 1936*, 3rd edition, Reykjavik, 1936.

Troil, Uno von, *Letters on Iceland . . . Made during a voyage undertaken in the Year 1772 by Joseph Banks, Esq., F.R.S.*, Dublin, 1780.

LITERATURE

Beck, Richard, *Icelandic Lyrics; Originals and Translations*, Reykjavik, 1930.

Carlyle, Thomas, *Heroes and Hero-Worship*, New York, 1881.

Craigie, Sir William, *The Icelandic Saga*, 2nd edition, Cambridge, 1933.

Dasent, George Webbe, op. cit.

—— *The Story of Burnt Njal*, 2 vols., Edinburgh, 1861.

Encyclopaedia Britannica, 14th edition, 1929.

Hall, Mrs A. W., *Icelandic Fairy Tales*, London, n.d.

Hermannsson, Halldor (compiler), *Catalogue of the Icelandic Collection Bequeathed by Willard Fiske*, Ithaca, N.Y., 1914.

—— *Catalogue of the Icelandic Collection Bequeathed by Willard Fiske, Additions 1913–26*, Ithaca and London, 1927.

Huntington, Ellsworth, *The Character of Races*, New York and London, 1927.

Ilbert, C. P., "Appendix to Chapter on Iceland," in Bryce, *Memories*, cited *post*.

Kirkconnell, Watson, op. cit.

Koht, Hvaldan, *The Old Norse Sagas*, New York, 1931.

Magnusson, Eirikr and William Morris, *The Story of the Volsungs and Niblungs with Certain Songs from the Elder Edda*, London, 1870.

ICELAND TODAY

Bryce, Viscount James, *Memories of Travel*, New York, 1923.

Lindroth, Hjalmar, *Iceland: a Land of Contrasts*, translated from the Swedish by Adolph Benson, New York, 1937.

Russell, W. S. C., *Iceland: Horseback Tours in Saga Land*, Boston, 1914.

Thorsteinsson, Thorsteinn, op. cit.

EDUCATION

Baring-Gould, S., *Iceland, Its Scenes and Its Sagas*, London, 1863.

Barrow, John Jr, *Visit to Iceland . . . in the "Flower of Yarrow" Yacht in the Summer of 1834*, London, 1835.

Chapman, Olive M., *Across Iceland*, London and New York, 1930.

Headley, P. C., *Island of Fire*, Boston, 1874.

Ilbert, C. P., op. cit.

Lindroth, Hjalmar, op. cit.

Mackenzie, Sir George Steuart, op. cit.

Ministry of Education, Reykjavik.

Taylor, Bayard, op. cit.

Thorsteinsson, Thorsteinn, op. cit.

MEDICAL SERVICES

Based on information chiefly from Ministry of Health, Reykjavik.

Health and Social Conditions

Based on information chiefly from Ministry of Health, Reykjavik; but also upon:

Anderson, Johann, *Nachrichten von Island*, Frankfort and Leipzig, 1747.

Horrebow, N., op. cit.

Mackenzie, Sir George Steuart, op. cit.

Thorsteinsson, Thorsteinn, op. cit.

Co-operative Movement in Iceland

Based mainly on information from the Federation of Co-operative Societies, Reykjavik; but also upon:

Baker, Joseph, *Co-operative Enterprise*, New York, 1937.

Olafsson, Ragnar, "Co-operative Iceland," in *The American Scandinavian Review*, Spring, 1939.

Agriculture

Based mainly on information received from the Ministry of Agriculture, Reykjavik.

Fisheries

Based mainly on information received from the State Bureau of Fisheries, Reykjavik.

Other Industries

Based mainly on information received from the Ministry of Commerce and Industry.

Commerce

Based mainly on information received from the Ministry of Commerce and Industry.

Communications

Based mainly on information received from the Ministry of Commerce and Industry; but also upon:
Morgunbladid, Reykjavik, dispatch of December 15, 1938.

Iceland for Tourists

Bryce, James, *Memories*, cited above.
Dufferin, Lord, *Letters from High Latitudes*, London, 1857.
Howell, Frederick W. W., *Icelandic Pictures*, New York, n.d.
Russell, W. S. C., op. cit.
Statourist, Reykjavik.

Icelanders in the Americas

Black, Charles E. Drummond, *The Marquess of Dufferin and Ava*, London, 1903.
Dufferin, Lord, op. cit.
Executive Document No. 48, Senate, First Session, 44th Congress, "Information in Relation to Alaska and Its Resources," Washington, 1876.
Federal Writers' Project, *North Dakota: A Guide to the Northern Prairie State*, Fargo, 1938.
Gjerset, Knut, op. cit.
Holme, J. G., *Icelanders in the United States*, America's Making Exposition, New York, 1921.
Kirkconnell, Watson, op. cit.
McWilliams, Margaret, *Manitoba Milestones*, Toronto and London, 1928.
Olafsson, Jon, *Report of the Icelandic Committee from Wisconsin on the Character and Resources of Alaska*, Washington, 1875.
Rogers, J. D., *A Historical Geography of the British Colonies*, Vol. V, "Canada," Part III, Oxford, 1911
Taylor, Vernon, personal communication.
Thorfinnson, Thorl., personal communication.

APPENDIX B

THE ICELANDIC medical profession has one general organization, the Medical Association of Iceland. There are two others, the Reykjavik Medical Association, which publishes monthly the official journal of the profession, *Laeknabladid* (Journal of the Medical Profession); and the Akureyri Medical Association. Of the three, the Reykjavik organization is considered the most influential. Dentists and veterinary surgeons have the Dentists' Association of Iceland, and the Association of Icelandic Veterinary Surgeons; pharmaceutical chemists have the Pharmaceutical Chemists' Association of Iceland, while dispensing chemists who are in the service of others have founded the Association of Dispensing Chemists in Iceland. Midwives have the Icelandic Midwives' Association and nurses the Association of Icelandic Nurses. These last two publish a monthly periodical, *The Midwives' Journal* and *The Nurses' Journal*. Except for the Akureyri Medical Association, committees of all the above are in Reykjavik.

APPENDIX C

TABLE I

CHIEF IMPROVEMENTS IN CULTIVATION 1895–1937

YEAR	Leveling of Homefields, Hectares	New Cultivation Homefields, Hectares	Gardens, ha.	Drainage Covered Drains, m.	Drainage Ditches, m³	Storage of Manure, m³	Fencing, kilom.	Barns Dry, m³	Barns Silo, m³
1895–1904	1,588	545					759		
1905–1914	2,735	769					3,747		
1915–1925	1,634	399	123.4	150.932		19,199	2,213		
1926	182	544	11.1	41.552	41.962	7,352	665		
1927	178	703	13.5	33.974	55.899	14,426	673		
1928	216	1,068	14.4	41.938	72.694	16,942	763		
1929	368	1,660	20.3	87.179	161.872	17,605	1,535	74,651	2,118
1930	308	1,466	12.4	54.242	98.894	10,045	1,295	86,837	2,719
1931	345	1,329	16.9	79.031	136.091	10,720	1,000	59,215	4,707
1932	445	1,101	48.8	105.765	175.330	9,187	480	28,784	1,920
1933	316	1,020	62.2	64.092	99.348	9,548	325	35,478	1,771
1934	363	986	48.6	75.746	117.155	14,810	465	75,492	2,967
1935	351	757	60.8	85.076	121.352	19,580	506	69,101	10,763
1936	299	647	156.5	76.820	175.330	13,217	422	88,474	7,069
1937	254		108.8	69.490	94.870	14,272	875	112,752	6,531

TABLE 2

Area of Cultivated Land and Yield

| | Cultivated Land Hectares | | Yield of Cultivated Land | | | |
	Homefield	Market Gardens	Hay from Homefields	Potatoes	Turnips	Hay from Wild Meadows
			100 Kilos.	100 Kilos.	100 Kg.	100 Kilos.
1900	17,837	249				
1901–1905 average			524,000	18,820	19,040	1.002000
1906–1910 average			536,000	24,060	14,580	1.059000
1910	18,591	325				
1911–1915 average			574,000	24,600	13,800	1.138000
1916–1920 average			513,000	28,580	12,440	1.176000
1920	22,031	453				
1921–1925 average			647,000	22,765	9,562	1.039000
1926–1930 average			798,000	39,737	14,403	1.032000
1930	26,184	455				
1931–1935 average			1,101,000	42,600	17,000	1.019000
1935	32,029	544	1,126,000	46,050	15,288	1.006000
1936	33,398	657	1,150,000	84,370	24,677	1.139000
1937	34,155	657	1,003,100	64,170	14,821	1.045705

TABLE 3

The Livestock of the Icelanders

(Total figures as compared with the population)

(*Livestock, in thousands*)

YEAR	CATTLE			SHEEP			HORSES			OTHER LIVESTOCK		
	Total	Per 100 Pers.		Total	Per 100 Pers.		Total	Per 100 Pers.		Poultry	Grazing Sheep	Furred Animals
		Relation to Total Number of Inhab.	Relation to Persons Living by Agriculture		Relation to Total Number of Inhab.	Relation to Persons Living by Agriculture		Relation to Total Number of Inhab.	Relation to Persons Living by Agriculture		Per 100 Pers.	Per 100 Pers.
1703	35.8	70		279.0	554		22.9	53				
1800	23.3	49	58	304.2	644	760	28.3	60	71			
1849	25.5	43	55	619.1	1,048	1,330	37.6	63	81			
1900	23.6	33	59	469.5	614	1,075	41.7	55	104			
1910	26.3	31	61	578.6	671	1,334	44.8	51	103		0.3	
1920	23.5	25	58	578.8	611	1,426	50.6	45	125	15.5		
1930	30.1	28	77	690.2	642	1,770	48.9	46	125	44.4	2.9	
1935	35.6	31	91	658.7	569	1,682	45.0	39	115	80.0	2.3	1.7
1936	37.0	32	95	656.1	561	1,700	46.0	40	120	86.9	2.1	1.8
1937	37.6	32	95	654.1	558	1,700	47.2	41	127	79.7	1.8	2.4

TABLE 4

Production of some of the chief agricultural produce 1901–1937

YEAR	POPULATION ENGAGED IN AGRICULTURE		PRODUCTION						PRODUCTION PER INHABITANT						VALUE OF THE AGRICULTURAL PRODUCE IN ICEL. KRONUR.
	Number	% of Population	Mutton 1000 kilos.	Other kinds of meat, 1000 kilos.	Milk 1000 kilos.	Wool 1000 kilos.	Potatoes and turnips 1000 kilos.	Eggs in thousands	Mutton, kilos.	Other meat, kilos.	Milk, kilos.	Wool, kilos.	Potatoes and Swedes, kilos.	Number of eggs	
1901	45,993	58.6	3,255	1,030	38,488	603	2,724	397	71	22	837	13	59	9	7.554.000
1905	44,702		3,841	1,126	40,890	679	4,123	397	86	25	915	15	92	9	8.364.000
1910	43,411	51.0	4,462	1,084	39,826	723	4,542	544	107	25	917	17	105	13	9.292.000
1915	42,013		2,370	1,005	40,843	695	4,251	921	128	24	972	17	101	22	16.334.000
1920	40,614	42.0	5,623	994	38,006	723	4,433	1,767	138	24	936	18	109	44	30.875.000
1925	39,809		5,772	1,115	45,761	707	4,623	2,512	145	28	1,150	18	116	63	30.082.000
1930	39,003	35.8	6,896	1,189	54,794	863	4,868	5,066	177	30	1,405	22	125	130	22.147.000
1934	39,900		7,418	1,302	59,899	874	6,417	8,442	190	33	1,536	22	165	216	24.307.000
1935	39,000		7,094	1,350	61,614	820	6,144	9,229	182	35	1,580	21	158	237	25.355.000
1936	39,000		6,964	1,400	65,449	817	10,895	9,791	178	36	1,678	21	279	251	28.459.000
1937	39,000		6,882	1,400	66,457	818	7,900	9,677	176	36	1,704	21	203	248	29.257.000

APPENDIX D

AMONG EUROPEAN countries we find Norway ranks first in quantity of fish caught in 1935, with some 10,366,000 tons. England comes next with 7,299,000 tons, while Germany and Scotland show 4,689,000 and 2,797,000 tons respectively. Immediately following these four great fishing powers, we find that little Iceland, with its 7000 fishermen, brought ashore 2,661,000 tons.

In order to get a better understanding of the meaning of these figures, we look at them from another point of view. If we analyze the production in terms of population, we get the following results:

Germans	15.4	lbs. per inhabitant
French	24.2	" " "
English	44.1	" " "
Scotch	70.5	" " "
Norwegians	815.8	" " "
Icelanders	5,104.5	" " "

These comparisons are based on figures given by International Fisheries Statistics.

APPENDIX E

TABLE 1: VALUE OF IMPORTS AND EXPORTS EXPRESSED IN ICELANDIC KRONUR

	Imports	Exports	Total Imports and Exports	Exports Surplus
1896–1900	5,966,000	7,014,000	12,980,000	1,048,000
1901–1905	8,497,000	10,424,000	18,921,000	1,927,000
1906–1910	11,531,000	13,707,000	25,238,000	2,176,000
1911–1915	18,112,000	22,368,000	40,480,000	4,256,000
1916–1920	53,709,000	48,453,000	102,162,000	5,256,000
1921–1925	56,562,000	64,212,000	120,774,000	7,560,000
1926–1930	64,853,000	66,104,000	130,957,000	1,251,000
1931–1935	46,406,000	48,651,000	95,057,000	2,245,000
1936	43,053,000	49,642,000	92,695,000	6,589,000
1937 (Provisional figures)	51,768,000	58,867,000	110,635,000	7,099,000

TABLE 2: CLASSIFICATION OF EXPORTS

(Values expressed in Icelandic kronur)

	Fish Products	Agricultural Products	Miscellaneous	Total Exports
1901–1905	6,178,000	2,192,000	2,054,000	10,424,000
1906–1910	8,823,000	2,986,000	1,898,000	13,707,000
1911–1915	16,574,000	5,091,000	703,000	22,368,000
1916–1920	36,147,000	10,879,000	1,428,000	48,454,000
1921–1925	54,664,000	8,445,000	1,093,000	64,211,000
1926–1930	58,072,000	7,319,000	713,000	66,104,000
1931–1935	43,473,000	4,636,000	542,000	48,651,000
1936	41,189,000	7,689,000	762,000	49,642,000

TABLE 3: ANALYSIS OF EXPORTS

		Quantity	Value (f.o.b.) 1000 kr.
Klipfish	Tons	25,210	12.339
Salted fish (uncured) . . .	"	13,564	3.667
Fresh fish (frozen)	"	15,119	4.785
Stock fish.	"	855	.455
Herring (cured)	Barrels	203,318	5.833
Cod-liver oil	Tons	4,611	4.145
Redfish oil	"	564	.330
Herring oil	"	21,419	8.678
Herring and other fishmeal .	"	31,372	6.585
Roes (salted).	Barrels	20,261	.775
Mutton (salted)	"	8,415	.794
Mutton (frozen)	Tons	2,215	2.213
Sheep casings	"	87	.481
Wool	"	727	2.955
Sheepskins (green, salted) .	Thousands	392	2.428
Sheepskins (unhaired) . . .	Tons	70	.294

TABLE 4: ANALYSIS OF IMPORTS

(Expressed in percentages)

	1913	1921–25	1926–30	1931–35
Food products	18.6	16.4	11.9	10.0
Luxuries	10.6	10.9	7.7	7.5
Manufactured goods and clothing	13.2	14.8	16.0	14.5
For domestic and personal use .	4.4	5.7	7.2	6.5
Fuel for light and heating . .	14.9	13.8	10.6	11.9
Building materials	6.5	7.8	10.3	9.9
Fisheries equipment	22.1	16.7	15.9	14.1
Agricultural equipment . . .	1.5	1.9	3.1	4.4
Miscellaneous	8.2	12.0	17.3	21.1

TABLE 5: ANALYSIS OF IMPORTS, CONSUMPTION GOODS AND CAPITAL GOODS

(Expressed in percentages)

	Consumption Goods	Capital Goods
1916–1920	46.8	53.2
1920–1925	47.9	52.1
1926–1930	42.8	57.2
1931–1935	38.6	61.4
1935	34.8	65.2
1936	31.1	68.9

TABLE 6: VALUE OF IMPORTS IN ICELANDIC KRONUR

	1937
Cereals	4,539,000
Fruits and vegetables	377,000
Colonial produce	2,112,000
Cloth and clothing	4,045,000
Footwear	1,057,000
Building and construction material	7,826,000
Shipping materials	15,691,000
Agricultural materials	1,152,000
Ships, vehicles, machinery	4,199,000
Tools, household utensils, etc.	1,592,000
Industrial raw materials	1,963,000
Sanitary goods	263,000
Books and stationery supplies	1,273,000
Musical instruments and leather goods	44,000
Electrical goods	2,008,000
Clocks, watches, jewelry	62,000
Monopolized goods (fertilizers)	683,000
Monopolized goods (wines, spirits, tobacco, radio)	1,779,000
Miscellaneous	2,636,000

TABLE 7: IMPORTS AND EXPORTS BY COUNTRIES

(*Expressed in percentages*)

	1918		1925		1930		1933		1936		1937[1]	
	Imp.	*Exp.*	*Imp.*	*Exp.*	*Imp.*	*Exp.*	*Imp.*	*Exp.*	*Imp.*	*Exp.*	*Imp.*	*Exp.*
Denmark	27	2	33.3	10.1	28.1	4.3	23.5	5.6	16.4	7.9	14.	9.
Gt. Britain	28	48	34.3	13.2	26.9	15.5	32.4	11.1	26.7	14.9	26.	17.
Norway	1	12	13.3	11.6	10.8	8.2	11.8	6.9	6.8	10.0	9.	12.
Sweden	3	0	2.6	8.1	4.8	6.2	4.3	4.1	10.4	8.1	10.	7.
Germany	0	0	5.7	1.7	15.9	8.2	13.0	8.6	21.9	16.5	21.	19.
Holland	0	0	2.1	0.3	2.2	0.2	1.7	1.2	1.0	2.7	1.	4.
Spain	8	19	4.1	40.5	3.2	34.0	4.9	28.8	4.1	2.7	1.	4.
Italy	0	2	0.6	9.8	0.2	12.6	0.8	12.2	5.5	5.7	9.	5.
Portugal	0	0	0.1	1.3	0.2	6.0	0.3	14.4	0.9	12.4	0.	10.
U.S.A.	33	15	2.0	0.3	3.2	2.6	1.5	4.1	1.2	11.0	2.	8.
Other countries	0	2	1.9	3.1	4.5	2.2	5.8	3.0	5.1	8.1	7.	8.

[1]Provisional figures.

050880